D1116540

■ **DRUGS**
The Straight Facts

Botox® and Other Cosmetic Drugs

DRUGS The Straight Facts

■ DRUGS
The Straight Facts

Botox®
and Other
Cosmetic
Drugs

Suellen May

Consulting Editor
David J. Triggle

University Professor
School of Pharmacy and Pharmaceutical Sciences
State University of New York at Buffalo

CHELSEA HOUSE
P U B L I S H E R S
An imprint of Infobase Publishing

Drugs The Straight Facts: Botox and Other Cosmetic Drugs

Chelsea House
An imprint of Infobase Publishing
132 West 31st Street
New York NY 10001

Library of Congress Cataloging-in-Publication Data
May, Suellen.
  Botox and other cosmetic drugs / Suellen May, David J. Triggle.
    p. cm. — (Drugs: the straight facts)
  Includes bibliographical references and index.
  ISBN-13: 978-0-7910-9776-2 (alk. paper)
  ISBN-10: 0-7910-9776-5 (alk. paper)
  1. Botulinum toxin—Popular works. 2. Cosmetics—Popular works. I. Triggle, D. J. II. Title. III. Series.

  RL120.B66M39 2008
  615'.329364—dc22

                                    2007050327

Chelsea House books are available at special discounts when purchased in bulk quantities for businesses, associations, institutions, or sales promotions. Please call our Special Sales Department in New York at (212) 967-8800 or (800) 322-8755.

You can find Chelsea House on the World Wide Web at
http://www.chelseahouse.com

Text and cover design by Terry Mallon and Keith Trego

Printed in the United States of America

Bang EJB 10 9 8 7 6 5 4 3 2

This book is printed on acid-free paper.

All links and Web addresses were checked and verified to be correct at the time of publication. Because of the dynamic nature of the Web, some addresses and links may have changed since publication and may no longer be valid.

Table of Contents

The Use and Abuse of Drugs

For thousands of years, humans have used a variety of sources with which to cure their ills, cast out devils, promote their well-being, relieve their misery, and control their fertility. Until the beginning of the twentieth century, the agents used were all of natural origin, including many derived from plants as well as elements such as antimony, sulfur, mercury, and arsenic. The sixteenth-century alchemist and physician Paracelsus used mercury and arsenic in his treatment of syphilis, worms, and other diseases that were common at that time; his cure rates, however, remain unknown. Many drugs used today have their origins in natural products. Antimony derivatives, for example, are used in the treatment of the nasty tropical disease leish-maniasis. These plant-derived products represent molecules that have been "forged in the crucible of evolution" and con-tinue to supply the scientist with molecular scaffolds for new drug development.

Our story of modern drug discovery may be considered to start with the German physician and scientist Paul Ehrlich, often called the father of chemotherapy. Born in 1854, Ehrlich became interested in the ways in which synthetic dyes, then becoming a major product of the German fine chemical industry, could stain selectively certain tissues and components of cells. He reasoned that such dyes might form the basis for drugs that could interact selectively with diseased or foreign cells and organisms. One of Ehrlich's early successes was development of the arsenical "606"—patented under the name Salvarsan—as a treatment for syphilis. Ehrlich's goal was to create a "magic bullet," a drug that would target only the diseased cell or the invading disease-causing organism and have no effect on healthy cells and tissues. In this he was not successful, but his great research did lay the groundwork for the successes of the twentieth century, including the discovery of the sulfonamides and the antibiotic penicillin. The latter agent saved countless lives during World War II. Ehrlich, like many scientists, was an optimist. On the eve of World War I, he wrote, "Now that the liability to, and danger of, disease are to a large extent circumscribed—the efforts of chemotherapeutics are directed as far as possible to fill up the gaps left in this ring." As we shall see in the pages of this volume, it is neither the first nor the last time that science has proclaimed its victory over Nature only to have to see this optimism dashed in the light of some freshly emerging infection.

From these advances, however, has come the vast array of drugs that are available to the modern physician. We are increasingly close to Ehrlich's magic bullet: Drugs can now target very specific molecular defects in a number of cancers, and doctors today have the ability to investigate the human genome to more effectively match the drug and the patient. In the next one to two decades, it is almost certain that the cost of "reading" an individual genome will be sufficiently cheap that, at least in the developed world, such personalized medicines will become the norm. The development of such drugs, however, is extremely costly and raises significant social issues, including equity in the delivery of medical treatment.

The twenty-first century will continue to produce major advances in medicines and medicine delivery. Nature is, however, a resilient foe. Diseases and organisms develop resistance to existing drugs, and new drugs must constantly be developed. (This is particularly true for anti-infective and anticancer agents.) Additionally, new and more lethal forms of existing infectious diseases can develop rapidly. With the ease of global travel, these can spread from Timbuktu to Toledo in less than 24 hours and become pandemics. Hence the current concerns with avian flu. Also, diseases that have previously been dormant or geographically circumscribed may suddenly break out worldwide. (Imagine, for example, a worldwide pandemic of Ebola disease, with public health agencies totally overwhelmed.) Finally, there are serious concerns regarding the possibility of man-made epidemics occurring through the deliberate or accidental spread of disease agents—including manufactured agents, such as smallpox with enhanced lethality. It is therefore imperative that the search for new medicines continues.

All of us at some time in our life will take a medicine, even if it is only aspirin for a headache or to reduce cosmetic defects. For some individuals, drug use will be constant throughout life. As we age, we will likely be exposed to a variety of medications—from childhood vaccines to drugs to relieve pain caused by a terminal disease. It is not easy to get accurate and understandable information about the drugs that we consume to treat diseases and disorders. There are, of course, highly specialized volumes aimed at medical or scientific professionals. These, however, demand a sophisticated knowledge base and experience to be comprehended. Advertising on television is widely available but provides only fleeting information, usually about only a single drug and designed to market rather than inform. The intent of this series of books, Drugs: The Straight Facts, is to provide the lay reader with intelligent, readable, and accurate descriptions of drugs, why and how they are used, their limitations, their side effects and their future. It is our hope that these books will provide readers with sufficient information to satisfy their immediate needs and to serve as an adequate base for further investigation and for asking intelligent questions of health care providers.

The present volume, *Botox and Other Cosmetic Drugs,* illustrates the way in which drugs can be used to reduce or eliminate "cosmetic" defects. Such defects can, in the more severe form, be psychologically disturbing and hence treatment becomes appropriate. Botox is an interesting example of how an extremely potent neurotoxin, derived from the anaerobic bacterium *Clostridium botulinum,* associated with often-lethal food poisoning, can be used to relax muscle activity. Hence, it can be used not only to relieve the muscle spasms seen in various conditions but also to reduce the frown lines and facial wrinkling typically associated with

aging. Regardless of whether such drugs are used for medi-
cally recognized disorders or solely for cosmetic purposes an
understanding of how and where they work is important.

David J. Triggle, Ph.D.
University Professor
School of Pharmacy and Pharmaceutical Sciences
State University of New York at Buffalo

Introduction: Cosmetics Versus Drugs—Defining the Difference

Drugs are compounds that affect the body and mind. Some drugs require a prescription and others can be purchased over the counter. The U.S. Food and Drug Administration (FDA) determines what a drug is, what a **cosmetic** is, and defines both in a law titled the Food, Drug, and Cosmetic Act.

At the mention of cosmetics, many might think of mascara, blush, or eye shadow. True, all are cosmetics as defined by the FDA. The FDA defines a cosmetic by its intended use. The FDA defines a cosmetic as an article intended to be rubbed, poured, sprinkled, sprayed on, or otherwise applied to the human body for cleansing, beautifying, or altering the appearance. The FDA defines a drug as a compound used for diagnosis, cure, mitigation, treatment, or prevention of disease. If a product falls into both categories, it is considered a **cosmetic drug**, also referred to as cosmetic medicine. A common cosmetic drug is a dandruff shampoo, since the product both cleans hair and treats dandruff, a medical condition. Sunscreen is a cosmetic drug because it is intended to prevent skin cancer as well as prevent an unsightly burn.

Cosmeceuticals is a term used by the cosmetics industry to refer to cosmetics that have medicinal benefits—mostly to improve skin, specifically to address wrinkles, acne, and pigmentation problems. The FDA does not address or define the term cosmeceuticals, and thus does not regulate cosmeceutical products, although many of these products are in fact cosmetic drugs such as Botox. This book focuses on cosmetic drugs and how these products affect the biological functioning of the human body.

COSMETICS: A HISTORICAL PERSPECTIVE

Throughout human history, people have used cosmetic treatments in an effort to attain their era's standard of beauty.

People in civilizations dating back many centuries have mixed potions and lotions to create a better appearance, improve health, and elevate their social stature. The early Egyptians used dyes to color their hair, skin, and nails. Kohl was a powder used to color the upper and lower lids to make the eyes appear more almond shaped. Kohl consisted of crushed metals and other compounds including copper and ash; it was believed to reduce eye infection and improve eyesight. Although kohl did not possess medicinal properties, oils and lotions used by Egyptians did protect the skin from harsh sunlight. Early people did not have labs to test their products, but in some cases they discovered products that are still used today.

Many of the chemicals found to be successful by earlier people still have some validity today. For example, the Chinese have long known the health benefits of green tea. Green tea contains helpful **antioxidants**, such as catechin and vitamin C, which help stave off the aging process. Antioxidants are chemicals that are believed to protect and repair the skin by boosting **collagen** production. They also strengthen blood vessels. Today green tea is a popular additive in antiaging creams.

ALOE VERA, ANTIOXIDANTS, AND CHEMICAL PEELS

Cut open a leaf of the aloe vera plant and a cooling gel will ooze out. This gel is commonly used to soothe burns. Although the plant grows naturally in African deserts, many people keep an aloe vera plant in the kitchen in case someone gets too close to a hot pan. To spread a little aloe vera on burned skin is to engage in an ancient practice dating back to the ancient Egyptians.

The ancient Egyptians, whose civilization dates back over 3,000 years, may not have had rigorous scientific testing as we have today, but clearly they were good observers and recorders—which are vital skills for scientists. Early Egyptian writings indicate that aloe vera was used to treat skin ailments, infections, and constipation. In ancient Greece, Alexander the Great provided aloe vera for his wounded soldiers.

What the early Egyptians observed, as we do today, is that the gel aids in healing. Skin healing is enhanced by increased blood flow and **cell** creation. Aloe vera dilates capillaries, which increases blood circulation and therefore aids healing of the wounded skin. It also protects the skin from ultraviolet radiation. The gel consistency of aloe vera extracts also protects the skin from infection-causing bacteria and other microbes. Remember that one of the functions of the skin is to protect the body from infection by keeping harmful bacteria out of the body. When the skin is damaged, harmful bacteria can invade and colonize. Therefore, it makes sense that a topical agent with an antibacterial component such as aloe vera applied to wounded skin would have a healing effect. Aloe vera is still used in many cosmetic products, particularly those that soothe skin after a sunburn.

Tea tree oil is another ancient cosmetic drug. Tea tree oil is created from the distillation of leaves from the *Melaleuca alternifolia* plant that is native to Australia. Australian aboriginals discovered the curative nature of this plant and used it to heal cuts as well as fungal ailments. Because of its antifungal and antimicrobial properties, tea tree oil is found in many natural products to ease athlete's foot, acne, dandruff, periodontal disease, eczema, psoriasis, boils, and lice. It's also used as a general antiseptic. As with any compound that causes a biological response, tea tree oil should be used with caution. Some evidence suggests that tea tree oil can influence hormones and possibly cause breast enlargement in boys.

Modern society was not the first to use chemicals to make the skin appear younger. Chemical peels have long been a popular way to rejuvenate skin by removing the outermost layer with acidic products. New cell growth from the peel gives one a rosy glow. In ancient Egypt, nobles used lactic acid to encourage new cell growth. In the Middle Ages, wine and tartaric acid were also used. Although wine is no longer used for chemical peels, the products used today are also acidic. Modern methods for doing chemical peels will be discussed in Chapter 4.

DEADLY BEAUTY

As with modern beauty treatments, some used in the past were not only ineffective but also harmful—or even deadly. The use of belladonna by Renaissance women to dilate the pupils was one such harmful treatment. Belladonna is one of the most toxic plants in the Western Hemisphere. *Bella donna* is Italian for "beautiful lady." Extracts from the belladonna plant can dilate the pupils, which can be a signal of sexual arousal. This signal may be subconsciously noted by others, who may respond by becoming more attracted. Renaissance ladies believed their appeal would be increased by creating a more sexually charged interaction. Belladonna has the side effect of blurry vision, and if enough of the extract is consumed, such as by eating too many of the plant's berries, a person can become blind, enter a coma, and eventually die.

All parts of the belladonna plant contain a toxic chemical compound referred to as an **alkaloid**. Alkaloids strongly affect the nervous system. The nervous system controls functions such as sweating, breathing, and heart rate. When an alkaloid is introduced to the body, it disrupts these important signals in the body, resulting in an irregular heartbeat and labored breathing from respiratory distress. Alkaloids are found naturally in certain plants and have been used historically as sedatives, poisons, and as an **antidote** to other poisons. Cocaine is an example of an alkaloid that can be isolated from the leaves of the coca plant. In addition to dilating pupils, alkaloids can cause hallucinations, blurred vision, loss of balance, and confusion.

Although belladonna is no longer used today to enhance attractiveness, a safe derivative is used in medicine. Visit an eye doctor's office and you may receive drops that dilate your pupils. This drug is a derivative of the same chemical compound—an alkaloid—that dilated the eyes of hopeful Renaissance ladies.

Belladonna was not the only drug applied to the body that was harmful. The ancient Greeks and Romans were the first

Figure 1.1   Belladonna (*Atropa belladonna*) is also known as deadly nightshade. *(© Karen Tweedy-Holmes/CORBIS)*

to create their own foundation makeup—composed largely of white lead and chalk. Unlike today, pale skin was the beauty ideal. Pale skin was seen as the complexion of the wealthy since they did not have to toil in the fields as most others did. As a result, products to create a lighter complexion were concocted. Unfortunately, the lead in the foundation often fatally poisoned the people who wore it. Later, in the seventeenth century, the pale look became unfashionable, as it was associated with staying inside to avoid the plague. Like women of more recent times, those of early civilizations had the challenge of keeping up with changing fashions.

MEN AND ANCIENT TIMES

Men of early civilizations also went to great lengths to acquire a desirable appearance. Men through the centuries have wanted to halt or reverse hair loss. Whereas women have been concerned with social stature and attracting a mate, men have wanted the image of power and fortitude that a full head of hair represented. Egyptian men nearly 3,500 years ago created concoctions to cure baldness. Fat from lions, crocodiles, and geese was combined with hedgehog quills, oil, and honey, and the mixture was slathered on a barren head. Even Hippocrates, the famous Greek doctor of the fifth century B.C., applied sheep urine to his scalp in hopes of bringing back his hair. Modern treatments for baldness will be discussed in Chapter 5.

FROM PAST TO PRESENT

One consistent aspect of cosmetic drugs from ancient times to the present is that there are always products people are willing to peddle that simply do not work. Sheep urine does not cure baldness, although surely there were many who claimed it did. It was just as likely that many men probably believed it truly did work; vanity is certainly not a characteristic exclusive to modern society.

Advances in science have improved our understanding of how aging and dermatological problems affect the skin and have led to safer, more effective treatments to enhance the skin's appearance and health. Many drugs cure skin diseases, such as acne and **rosacea**, or improve the facial volume through fillers. Even so, there are plenty of "sheep urine" treatments out there. Today, hundreds of creams claim to cure cellulite, yet little scientific evidence supports these claims. These treatments will be examined in Chapter 4. In the end, only science in the form of experiments with consistent, repeatable results can determine a drug's validity.

1

Skin and Aging

The skin is an organ, just as the heart and lungs are organs. Skin also happens to be the largest organ. The function of the skin is to protect the body from harmful bacteria and light, and to regulate body temperature. If the skin becomes damaged to the extent that it can no longer protect the body, as is the case with burn victims, infection becomes a serious threat to one's survival.

LAYERS OF THE SKIN

Skin has three layers. The outermost layer is the **epidermis**, which is about as thick as a piece of paper. Hair emerges from the epidermis. The epidermis also contains pores and the oldest cells of the skin. These skin cells become dry and flake off and are replaced by newer cells. Children can count on a new layer of skin every month. As a person ages, the body does not replace skin cells as quickly. As a result, the skin layer becomes thinner.

The **dermis** is the dense layer of tissue beneath the epidermis; these two layers are tightly connected by a membrane. The dermis is much thicker than the epidermis and varies in thickness from 0.5 millimeters on the eyelid to 1.5 millimeters on thicker areas such as the back. The dermis cushions the body from strain and contains collagen and flexible, resilient connective tissue called **elastic fibers**. These elastic fibers are important to skin maintaining a youthful, taut appearance. They are also crucial in the body when tissues and organs need to expand and contract, such as when the heart pumps blood. The dermis is where the hair follicles, sweat glands, oil glands, and blood vessels lie.

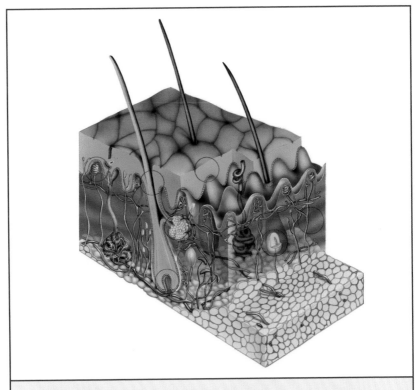

Figure 1.2 In this cross-section of the skin you can see the three main layers: the epidermis *(orange)*, the dermis, and the subcutaneous layer *(yellow)*. Also visible are the hair follicles and the sweat glands *(blue)*, nerves, blood vessels, and sebaceous gland. *(© Sophie Jacopin / Photo Researchers, Inc.)*

Underneath the dermis is the third layer —a fatty region referred to as the **subcutaneous layer**. The subcutaneous layer lies below the dermis, and its main function is to connect the skin to the underlying bone and muscle. The thickness of subcutaneous layer varies in people, depending on how much fat they have and the area of the body. Women tend to have a thicker subcutaneous layer near the thighs and buttocks, whereas men have a thicker layer in the abdomen.

The subcutaneous layer is also where the dimply deposits of cellulite reside. The cellulite exists between the connective layers in a pattern similar to a down quilt. The depth of the subcutaneous layer—deep enough to make topical penetration difficult and shallow enough for fat deposits to be seen—is the main difficulty with the presence and treatment of cellulite.

THE AGING PROCESS

Like all organs, the skin is made up of cells. Cells are the basic unit of living things. There are hundreds of different types of cells. Cells differ based on appearance and function. Immune cells fight disease. Nerve cells transmit information. Cells of the skin provide a structural framework and fight to keep harmful bacteria out of the body. Skin also regulates temperature; perspiring is a way for the overheated body to be cooled by emitting sweat to the skin surface. Blood vessels in the skin also dilate to dissipate heat when the body is hot. A person who appears red in the face from exercising probably has dilated blood vessels.

Like other cells, skin cells have a limited life span, but the body can create new ones. As skin ages, cell regeneration slows down. As cell regeneration slows down, the skin becomes thinner. Older skin tends to become damaged more easily and heal less quickly. Aging also leads to a decline in skin elasticity due to damage to elastic fibers in the skin. The results of skin aging are sagging and wrinkles. Skin aging occurs from two main processes: slowing cell regeneration and external triggers, primarily sunlight.

ULTRAVIOLET RADIATION AND SKIN DAMAGE

The following story is an example of how little thought many people give to tanning and the skin damage it causes:

> It's almost spring break and 20-year-old Charlotte is elated about going to Cancún with her friends. After all those exams, she's looking forward to hanging out with friends and soaking up the rays, particularly after such

a long winter in Missouri. Charlotte packs her bag and tosses in a bottle of suntan lotion with a very low sun protection factor (SPF) of 2 and baby oil. With her fair skin, she knows she'll burn a bit in the beginning but will later tan more easily. As long as she doesn't burn too badly, she figures she will be fine. Each time she spends too much time in the sun her mother admonishes her, but Charlotte just shrugs it off. She looks good now; she'll worry about wrinkles later.

Charlotte's carefree attitude is not unusual. Her tanning is a response from her cells to produce a pigment, referred to as **melanin**, as protection from ultraviolet radiation. Melanin is a pigment that causes the skin to tan; the more melanin you have, the darker the skin appears. It's important to note that the cells detect the damage and producing melanin is a defense. Individuals with darker skin naturally have more melanin and are therefore more protected from the sun's harmful rays. Unfortunately, Charlotte's consistent exposure to UV damages her skin and increases her chances of getting skin cancer. UV radiation is the main cause of skin cancer, and according to the National Cancer Institute, 40 to 50 percent of people who live to be 65 will have skin cancer once.

The type of UV exposure also affects the severity of cell damage. UV radiation, emitted by the sun as well as artificial sources, is divided into categories based on the size of the wavelengths. Shorter wavelengths cause greater damage to the skin. UVC is the shortest; UVB is the middle, and UVA—which is visible light—is the longest. Most of the UVC and UVB rays from the sun travel such a long distance that most of them do not reach the Earth's surface. Of the radiation that does reach the Earth's surface, more than 95 percent is UVA.

Sunlight damages skin because the light energy reacts with the skin cells, causing a breakup of chemical bonds. When the chemical bonds are broken, cell membranes can become damaged within even a few minutes of sun exposure, particularly if the light is richer in UVB rays than UVA rays. Over time, a person who has exposed his or her skin cells to too much ultraviolet radiation will suffer damage to the skin cells' **DNA (deoxyribonucleic acid)**, which can affect the person's health. The DNA within a cell has all the genetic instructions or "directions" for what a cell should do. Destroying a cell's DNA can enable it to behave in a manner different from its purpose, such as by growing uncontrollably. This is what happens in skin cancer, the most common cancer in the United States.

In terms of the skin's appearance, the sunlight also damages collagen and elastin fibers. This skin damage might not be immediately apparent to the naked eye, but the cumulative effect will result in premature aging such as wrinkles and loss of elasticity.

THE EFFECTS OF AGING ON THE SKIN

Aging slows cell rejuvenation. The elastic fibers in the dermis become damaged over a person's lifetime by sun exposure or aging. The dermis begins to produce an excessive number of abnormal fibers, which are denser or coarser. The fibers in young skin are able to "snap" the face back after smiling, chewing, squinting, or animating the face in any way. Damaged fibers do not have this same level of elasticity and therefore sag. It's similar to a rubber band that's been stretched too often and loses its elasticity. Interestingly, a person who stayed in the dark his or her entire life (without any sun exposure) would eventually develop wrinkles, although these wrinkles probably wouldn't appear until around 70 years of age. Wrinkles from sun damage, however, can appear as early as age 30.[3]

Skin with less elasticity tends to sag and wrinkle, particularly in areas of the face that are more frequently creased by facial movements. "Smoker's mouth" is characterized by deeply grooved lines around the mouth from the constant puckering of smoking. Often as people age, a fold develops vertically going from the nose to the chin; this fold is referred to as a nasolabial fold and is caused by a loss of skin elasticity.

The question that most people have after learning about these effects is, "How can this be avoided or even reversed?" The most obvious answer is to minimize exposure to the sun

INDOOR TANNING: HARMLESS OR HAZARDOUS?

No amount of indoor tanning is healthy. Although a complete lack of sunlight could cause a vitamin D deficiency and rickets, it is rare. Even consistent use of a sunscreen at SPF 15 would enable the body to get enough sunlight to prevent a vitamin D deficiency.

Despite the warnings of skin cancer from ultraviolet radiation (UV) exposure, indoor tanning is a growing industry in the United States. Tanning beds generally emit mostly UVA, which is less damaging than UVB, although they also emit some UVB. UVA penetrates deeply into the skin, and mounting research indicates that, like UVB, UVA is a carcinogen. This means it can alter the DNA of skin cells, resulting in skin cancer.[1] Other health risks of indoor tanning include skin or corneal burns, cataract formation, and photoaging, which is aging of the skin from the sun.

Indoor tanning is very popular with fair-skinned, female teenagers, even more so if one of their parents tans. In addition, people who use tanning booths are more likely to be sunbathers, thus increasing their lifetime likelihood of getting skin cancer. Like drug manufacturers, manufacturers of indoor tanning equipment are regulated by the FDA. The FDA requires a limit on the amount of UV exposure a patron can receive. However a study in North Carolina showed that limits were exceeded by 95 percent of patrons without objection by the salon owners.[2]

The more you tan, the more you damage your skin cells' DNA, leading to premature aging and possibly skin cancer. A healthier way to get that bronzed look would be to apply a sunless tanner, preferably one with an SPF if you will be in the sun.

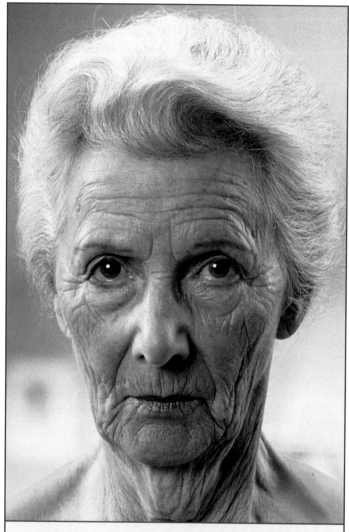

Figure 1.3 As skin ages it loses elasticity, which leads to sagging, wrinkles, and changes in the skin's texture. *(© G. Baden/zefa/CORBIS)*

and wear an ample amount of broad-spectrum sunscreen (which will block both UVA and UVB rays) when in the sun, as well as wearing protective clothing. Unfortunately, much of the damage from the sun occurs when we are younger and more concerned with the discomforts of sunburn than with wrinkles. However, even for those who blundered in their youth by lying out in the sun with oil, some cosmetic drugs are available to help improve the appearance of sun-damaged skin.

2

Botox: Beauty from Toxins

In 1990, Dr. Jean Carruthers, an observant ophthalmologist working in San Francisco, was using Botox to treat two medical conditions: spastic eye muscles and misaligned eyes. Dr. Carruthers treated the spastic eye muscles with injections of Botox near the eyebrows. She happened to notice her patients had fewer wrinkles around the brows after treatments. One of her patients also noticed the smoother appearance of her skin. The patient approached the doctor requesting more injections in the brow area. Dr. Carruthers told her she wouldn't do an injection because the area wasn't spasming. The patient said, "I know it's not spasming, but every time you treat me there I get this beautiful, untroubled expression."[4]

Like many medical advances, the use of Botox as a cosmetic drug was discovered by accident. It was apparent that Botox worked to prevent the wrinkling of the forehead. Dr. Carruthers knew that she had to prove her findings through repeated experiments with consistent results. Even though Botox was a drug approved to treat spastic eye muscles, she could not promote the **off-label** use of Botox as a treatment for wrinkles unless she could show consistent results from patients with repeated experiments.

THE MAKING OF A DRUG

Although it was clear to Dr. Carruthers and her patient that Botox was reducing wrinkles, she still had to prove it with research. Other doctors were also noticing this added benefit of Botox and were also formulating research.

From 1987 to 1990, Dr. Carruthers enrolled 30 patients to participate in Botox treatments on their wrinkles. Research on drugs is often a long process, lasting years or even decades, and all of the findings have to be carefully recorded. Once Dr. Carruthers was finished with her research, she presented her findings to other doctors at a meeting of the American Society for Dermatology in 1991 that took place in Florida. She then published her findings in the *Journal of Dermatologic Surgery and Oncology.* According to Dr. Carruthers, many of her colleagues thought injecting the face with Botox to reduce wrinkles was a crazy idea that was likely to go nowhere. Dr. Carruthers persisted, and in 2002 Botox was approved by the FDA for the treatment of wrinkles in the United States.

BOTOX VERSUS BOTULISM

At the mention of Botox, many people respond, "Isn't that a toxin?" It's true; Botox contains an inactive (nonliving) form

GOING "OFF-LABEL": IS IT LEGAL?

The term *off-label* refers to a drug being used for a purpose not approved by the FDA. Although the FDA states a specific purpose for any drug it approves, it is legal for physicians to use their own judgment when using a drug in a way that is not specifically listed on the label. For example, Botox was originally prescribed to treat crossed eyes, but then was used to treat wrinkles before the FDA approved it for that purpose.

Myobloc is the trade name of a drug similar to Botox. Although Myobloc's label states that it is intended for the treatment of cervical dystonia (involuntary muscle contractions in the neck and shoulder), it was used off-label for cosmetic purposes before it was approved for cosmetic use. The disadvantage of off-label use is that its effectiveness has not been proven, so a patient would need to trust his or her doctor to feel comfortable.

of **botulinum toxin A**, the same toxin responsible for **botulism**. Botulism is a life-threatening illness caused by eating food contaminated with the bacterium *Clostridium botulinum*. This bacterium occurs naturally in soil and marine sediment, and on the surfaces of fruits, vegetables, and seafood. Once a person eats the contaminated food, the bacteria multiply in his or her stomach and intestines. Bacteria populations increase at an exponential rate. This means that a small amount of bacteria can produce a relatively high population very quickly. The danger with *C. botulinum* is from the toxin it produces. *C. botulinum* produces several toxins, including botulinum toxin A, which is one of the most lethal toxins in the world.

At first, a person's body can handle a few *C. botulinum* bacteria secreting a small amount of the toxin. However, as the bacteria begin to multiply in the intestines, the amount of toxin produced overall becomes significantly greater and the person feels ill, usually within 18 to 36 hours. Because the toxin is being produced in the person's intestines, it is able to enter the bloodstream and affect the entire body. Botulism begins with cranial nerve paralysis, but eventually all of the muscles of the body will become paralyzed. The most critical muscles affected are the ones used to breathe. People who die of botulism usually suffocate because the respiratory muscles no longer function. There are several ways that the *C. botulinum* bacteria can find their way into the body, and each causes severe reactions. Understanding how the toxin produced by this bacteria works in its active form can help you better understand how the cosmetic drug Botox works.

Foodborne Botulism

A frightening case of foodborne botulism was reported in the *Canadian Journal of Anesthesia*. A healthy 35-year-old man was having dinner with his family at a local restaurant. His meal was served with a foil-wrapped baked potato. He took one bite and spat out the foul-tasting potato. He continued eating the rest of his meal without giving it much more

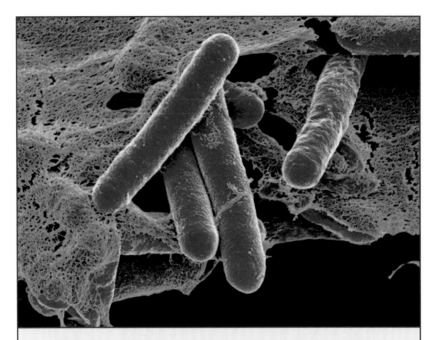

Figure 2.1 *Clostridium botulinum* bacteria.*(© Gary Gaugler / Visuals Unlimited)*

thought. He woke approximately 12 hours after his dinner feeling sick with a stomachache and blurred vision. He began to feel worse and suspected the potato. Three hours later he was taken to the hospital in an ambulance. In addition to the blurred vision, his muscles were weak and he had difficulty breathing. His condition continued to decline and his trachea was intubated, meaning that a tube was placed into the trachea and his lungs were ventilated so that he could breathe. A little later he had no cranial nerve function. Cranial nerves control major functions such as turning eyes from side to side, chewing, swallowing, and vision. He also had little muscle control over his legs and arms.

The patient let the doctors know about the potato; because of his increasing paralysis, botulism was suspected. Unfortunately the potato was not available to test. The doctors decided to treat the patient on the assumption that he had botulism, and he was given an antitoxin. He experienced no further neurological decline after receiving the antitoxin. Twelve days later, blood samples from the patient tested positive for the toxin that causes botulism. The man required extensive rehabilitation in the intensive care unit of the hospital. It took six and a half months for him to be released from the hospital. Luckily, he did not need long-term care.[5]

Botulism from Improper Canning

Food spoils because of microorganisms. Contaminated food, even food contaminated with the *C. botulinum* toxin, may not look or smell spoiled. One way to preserve food safely is proper canning. Canning forces all of the air from the jar, thus creating a vacuum and preventing microorganisms from entering and spoiling food. In the 1970s, there was an outbreak of botulism from improper canning. Botulism scares still occur today. In 2006, Excelsior Foods recalled olives distributed in Canada due to concerns about *C. botulinum*. In July 2007, canned hot dog chili sauce caused four people—two from Texas and two from Indiana—to go to the hospital with botulism. All four people were expected to survive. The FDA sent experts to the canning plant to determine what went wrong.

Since the 1970s, these four cases are the only known incidents of botulism from commercially canned foods. Today, botulism cases are still reported, but they are usually a result of improper canning done at home.

Bacteria cause food spoilage. During the canning process, air is driven from the jar and a vacuum is formed as the jar cools and seals, preventing microorganisms from entering and recontaminating the food. Boiling or heating food is also critical. Ideally, heating will kill bacteria already on food, but the right temperature is critical. A jar can be sealed, but some of the bacteria could still be alive unless the food was boiled for long enough. The acidity of the food determines how high the temperature must get before canning to kill all of the bacteria.

Lower-acidity foods, such as vegetables, meats, poultry, and fish, must be heated to higher temperatures than higher-acidity foods, such as tomatoes. Many of the cases of botulism from home-canned foods occur with low-acid foods. Foods that have a higher acidity level inhibit the growth of *C. botulinum* bacteria or at least make it easier to destroy the bacteria by heating. Acidic foods need to be heated to 250°F. Low-acid foods require a pressure canner to reach temperatures high enough to kill all bacteria. If all of the bacteria are not killed and the can is opened at a later date, even a taste of the food could be fatal.

Infant Botulism

Unlike foodborne botulism, infant botulism occurs when a baby ingests the spores of *C. botulinum* and the live bacteria begin to grow. In an adult or older child with a more mature digestive system, these spores would be passed through the digestive system without causing harm; however, in a baby's intestines these spores can develop into bacteria that produce a potentially lethal toxin.

The bacteria responsible for infant botulism are not always the same as those responsible for foodborne botulism. In rare cases, two bacteria closely related to *C. botulinum* can also cause infant botulism; they are *Clostridium butyricum* and *Clostridium baratii*. All of these species of bacteria produce a lethal toxin. The toxins produced by the bacteria can also vary. *C. botulinum* produces seven types of toxins designated by letters A through G. Infant botulism can be caused by the same bacteria that produce the toxin in Botox (A), or by toxins B, E, or F.

No matter which bacteria or toxin is responsible for a case of infant botulism, the symptoms are the same—a paralyzing effect on the body that can prevent a baby from breathing, moving, and eating. An infant with botulism must be treated in a hospital and must be given assisted breathing until the effects of the toxin wear off.

Honey is the most common source of infant botulism. Honey may contain minute amounts of *C. botulinum*,

C. butyricum, or *C. baratii* that occur naturally in the soil. The infant botulism that can result from contaminated honey is suspected to be a possible cause of **sudden infant death syndrome (SIDS)**. This is why pediatricians recommend that infants not be fed honey.

Botulism from Fermentation

Alaska has a higher rate of botulism than other states; approximately 27 percent of U.S. foodborne botulism cases occur there, according to the Centers for Disease Control and Prevention (CDC).[6] Alaska native tradition incorporates fermentation in food preparation. Bear paws, blubber, and seal flippers are fermented to be eaten later. Traditionally, these foods were fermented in a grass-lined hole or wooden barrel in the ground. But starting in the 1970s, these foods were fermented aboveground in glass or plastic. With this newer practice, botulism cases increased due to the warmer temperatures and anaerobic (oxygen-free) conditions that are favorable to the growth of *C. botulinum*. Once *C. botulinum* is allowed to grow and contaminate the meat with the toxin, the food will remain toxic despite freezing, although thorough cooking can destroy it. Antitoxins and emergency medical plans are in place throughout the Arctic to help handle the occasional outbreak.

Botulinum Type C

In 2004, 14 waterfowl died at a city-owned recreational lake in Las Cruces, New Mexico. Residents were horrified, and city officials and the New Mexico Department of Game and Fish quickly began working together to close the lake and discover the cause of the deaths. Samples taken from the lake and examined showed the cause of death for the waterfowl to be a type of botulism due to poor conditions of the lake.

Type C botulism is associated with marine life. It develops in shallow waters, where there are conditions that promote bacterial growth, including a lot of decaying vegetation and higher water temperatures. *C. botulinum* is naturally occurring in marshes, but for reasons not fully understood it is more common in some marshes than others.

Animals that live near marshes may eat the bacterial spores in their food without becoming ill. When these animals die, however, the spores will be in an ideal situation for germinating bacteria: low oxygen, warm temperatures, and high nutrients. These spore-producing bacteria create the deadly toxin that found its way to the ducks. Although waterfowl do not eat dead animals, they eat maggots, which feed on dead animals. The maggots had absorbed the deadly toxin from these dead animals. While the toxin may not affect the maggots, the birds can become ill if they consume a lot of the maggots that contain the bacteria. When a bird becomes infected with the botulism bacteria, it will often lose control of its neck muscles and drown. Once the bird has died, it provides more opportunity for scavenger insects to become tainted with the toxin, leading to the death of even more waterfowl, which eat those insects. This cycle is amplified as more and more birds die from eating the toxic insects. Each carcass has the ability to kill many birds; therefore thousands of birds end up dying from an initial infestation.

THERAPEUTIC USES FOR BOTOX

Whether it is used therapeutically or cosmetically, poisoning from a typical dose of Botox does not happen under normal circumstances because the botulinum toxin A in Botox is purified, meaning that no part of the Botox solution that is injected contains living bacteria. Since Botox contains no living organisms, the concentration of the toxin can't increase. The amount of toxin injected is very small in comparison to the amount needed for a lethal dose. In the case of botulism, the bacteria are alive in the body, which causes the toxin to increase to lethal levels. Another way to think of it is that a Botox injection contains a limited amount of toxin, which has been purified, restricting its effect to the areas close to the injection.

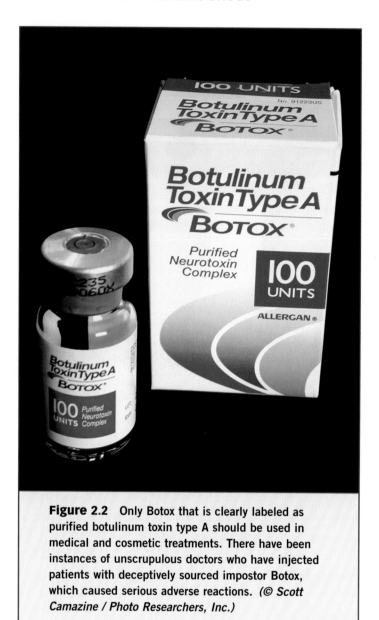

Figure 2.2   Only Botox that is clearly labeled as purified botulinum toxin type A should be used in medical and cosmetic treatments. There have been instances of unscrupulous doctors who have injected patients with deceptively sourced impostor Botox, which caused serious adverse reactions. *(© Scott Camazine / Photo Researchers, Inc.)*

Although Botox is most associated with wrinkles by the general public, the combined uses of Botox for other treatments is considerable. According to Allergan, the maker of

Botox, sales for cosmetic use were $357 million in 2005; thera-
peutic uses, however, surpassed those sales for a total of $473
million in 2005. Botox is used to treat the symptoms of disorders such as tension headaches, Parkinson's disease, cerebral
palsy, writer's cramp, excessive sweating, overactive bladder,
and scars. The common trait of all of these disorders is there is
some sort of muscle contraction or overstimulation. Excessive
sweating, for instance, is caused by overstimulation of sweat
glands that is triggered by **acetylcholine**, the **neurotransmitter**
that Botox inhibits. With all of these disorders, Botox treats
only the symptoms, not the underlying cause. Therefore injections must be repeated because the Botox will dissipate in the
body and eventually stop paralyzing the muscles causing the
overstimulation. For those who have tried the off-label uses of
Botox, these injections can have a life-changing impact.

Easing Vocal Cords

Diane Rehm is the host of a talk show on National Public
Radio covering current political and social issues, which airs
nationwide on local public radio stations. Listen closely and
you hear a halting quiver in her voice. It's slight but always
present. Diane Rehm suffers from spasmodic dysphonia, which
is a disease where the vocal cords clench, causing the voice to
quiver and crack. Without Botox, Diane Rehm's radio career
would have ended. She has Botox injected into her vocal chords
every four months and the clenching diminishes greatly.

Stopping Excessive Sweating

Brian is a bartender at a trendy Los Angeles club who was fea-
tured on the reality series *Dr. 90210*. Brian tried everything from
powders to deodorants to control his excessive sweating before
finally resigning himself to changing his sweat-soaked shirts
throughout the day. Then one day a friend of Brian's, Dr. Will
Kirby, noticed his perpetually wet armpits and suggested Botox.

The procedure is relatively simple, but a precise injection
is critical to maximize effectiveness. To properly pinpoint

the sweat glands, Brian's armpits are shaved and powder and iodine are applied. As the perspiration occurs, the substances mix and turn purple. The purple spots are where the Botox is injected in each armpit. Brian will see results in three to four days and results should last six to seven months. During this time, he probably won't sweat at all in the injected areas and won't even need antiperspirant or deodorant.

Relieving Chronic Headaches

Some unfortunate people experience chronic daily headaches and have tried almost everything to get relief—muscle relaxers, prescription narcotics, pain clinics, and even acupuncture. Some of these people finally find relief by getting Botox injections.

The doctor begins the procedure with injections in the middle of the forehead. Subsequent injections fan out from the forehead to the top of the ears. Some even get them on the back of the neck and halfway down the shoulder blades to relax the tense muscles that can cause headaches.

Patients often feel relief from their headaches within two weeks; this relief usually lasts two to six months before they need to go back for further injections. Doctors believe it is the muscles tightening in the back of the head that cause many of these severe headaches. The cost can be quite expensive, ranging from $350 to $1,200, depending on how many areas receive the injections. Insurance pays for neither Botox treatments to relieve migraines nor for Botox's cosmetic purposes. Despite the cost, most patients who have tried the procedure feel that it is worth it since it enables them to function.

Minimizing Scars

Scientists from the Mayo Clinic conducted research for seven years to prove that Botox can help reduce scarring if injected while a wound is healing. The Mayo Clinic is well known for its treatment of cancer; many patients undergo cancer surgery and are left with scarring. These large scars are the result of muscles pulling the wound apart slightly during healing. The botulinum toxin can weaken the muscles surrounding the scar if injected in the right locations. The affected muscles become immobilized and are not able to tug at the skin around the wound, which allows the area to heal more easily. Scarring is minimized if Botox is injected during the first two to four months of healing, and there is no need for repeated injections. Researchers at the Mayo Clinic were excited about the finding since there are no medications currently available that are scientifically proven to minimize scarring. Although these experiments had promising results, Botox has not yet been approved by the FDA for the treatment of wound scarring.

HOW BOTOX TREATS WRINKLES

So how does a Botox injection treat wrinkles? The face has one main nerve fiber that starts at the base of the skull with 7,000 individual nerve fibers that branch off from this main nerve fiber. Each nerve fiber controls a facial muscle with a unique function—such as smiling, squinting, or chewing. The botulinum toxin A in Botox paralyzes specific nerves that control facial muscles. The toxins attach to nerve endings and prevent the neurotransmitter from triggering muscle contractions. A neurotransmitter is a chemical that communicates information between nerve cells, or neurons. Without the neurotransmitter, the information cannot be exchanged and the muscle is unable to move.

Botox begins to take effect in four to seven days and wears off in three to four months, although longer-lasting results are reported with continued use, in some cases up to a year. Larger doses will yield more muscle paralysis and therefore longer-lasting control, but with the obvious disadvantage of too much paralysis, making the face look awkward. Where does the toxin go after the effect wears off? According to Allergan, the makers of Botox, the small amount of toxin is absorbed harmlessly into the body.

Botox is intended for muscles whose paralysis will not interfere with normal facial function, and it can ease only those wrinkles that are caused by facial movement. (Fillers are used for wrinkles and lines not caused by facial movement. They will be discussed in Chapter 3.) Typically, Botox is used for wrinkles around the eyes, referred to as crow's feet, vertical frown lines that occur between the eyebrows, and the horizontal lines of the forehead. In general, Botox works best for wrinkles above the nose, whereas fillers are meant for areas below the nose.

The number of nerve fibers in the wrinkled area plays a significant role in how quickly the effect will wear off. The more nerve fibers, the more quickly the paralyzing effect wears off. The areas around the eyes have more nerve endings close to muscle fibers; the tugging occurs more quickly there than on other areas of the face where there are fewer nerve endings close to muscles, such as between the eyes. As a result, a patient getting injections will see her crow's feet return before her frown lines do.

A big bonus of Botox injections is that the paralysis of the facial muscles stimulates collagen production. Collagen is a long, fibrous protein that provides structure to cells that make up skin, cartilage, tendons, and bone. Collagen adds volume to the face. As a person ages, collagen production decreases, which causes the skin to sag and wrinkle. When the skin is injected with Botox, the muscle no longer tugs on it, and this provides a better opportunity for the collagen to grow without its structure being affected by muscle contractions.

Botox must be injected to be successful. If applied to the skin, the toxin would not be able to penetrate the layers of the skin and still have the same effect as a Botox injection. To those who understand how the toxin works, this likely seems obvious. However, to the average consumer, who might not be as well educated about Botox, it may not. Hence the availability of creams such as Serutox and Wrinkle Relax, which claim to have the same benefits of Botox without the painful injections. These products contain peptides, the building blocks of proteins, which have long been claimed to control wrinkles. Dr. Leslie Baumann, the University of Miami's director of cosmetic dermatology, has reviewed the research behind these creams;

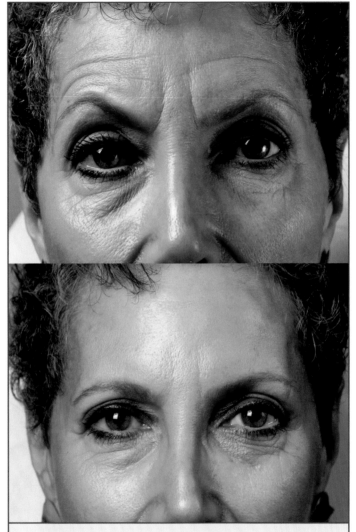

Figure 2.3 Here is a woman before *(top)* and after *(bottom)* receiving Botox injections. *(©Tannen Maury / The Image Works)*

she opines that these creams simply cannot paralyze muscles in the same way Botox can because the peptides would get sucked into the blood supply way before reaching the muscle.[7]

BOTOX PARTIES

One growing way of treating many people at once with Botox is at a Botox party. This story describes a typical Botox party:

> Alicia sits with a group of middle-aged women in a gated community in Southern California. Excited and just a little nervous, they eat appetizers in the living room of their neighbor. Cocktails are served as they wait for the doctor to show up to give them injections of Botox.
>
> This is Alicia's first time at a Botox party. She's never received treatments before, but at age 35, a few sidelong glances at the mirror reveal the lines fanning out from her eyes. She regrets all those trips to the tanning booth. Alicia had read over the pamphlets on Botox and understood that if treatments started early enough, before a deep-etched wrinkle was formed (versus a fine line), she would be able to look much younger in her older years.
>
> Alicia carefully sips a cocktail and waits for the doctor to call her name. She signs a waiver but neglects to check for the doctor's credentials. The doctor asks Alicia to squint, frown, and smile to associate the lines of her face with the muscles he will paralyze with Botox. The doctor injects about one-tenth of a teaspoon of the toxin into the muscles in the forehead and around the eyes. Within a couple minutes, Alicia is done. She rejoins the group and the next person is called to get her injections.

Botox parties are legal but controversial. As long as the individual administering Botox is licensed, it is acceptable to go to patients' homes or invite patients to a mass gathering such as a party. The FDA is concerned that the atmosphere of a social event diminishes the fact that a Botox injection is a surgical procedure and reduces the patient's perception of the seriousness of the situation.

Botox parties are also popular all over Europe.[8] In Italy, where new patients receive an introductory injection in the comfort of their host's home, these parties are the latest

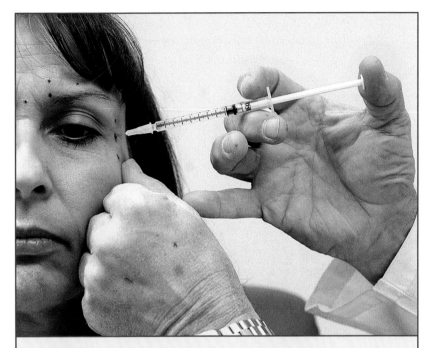

Figure 2.4 Botox needs to be injected in several places around the face to paralyze the muscles that cause wrinkling. This patient's face is marked with the numerous injection sites. (© AP Images)

fashion. This first injection is offered for free to entice the recipient in the hopes that he or she will come back for regular treatments.

Even when Botox is not injected at a party, the ease of application is part of its popularity. Patients can go to a clinic, get an injection over a lunch hour, and be back in the office without the discomfort or extreme swelling often associated with other cosmetic procedures.

INCREASING BOTOX'S EFFECTIVENESS

With many drugs, a tolerance can develop with repeated use. With Botox, however, the opposite is true, according to Dr. Michael Kane, author of *The Botox Book*.[9] Patients who consistently get Botox injections see longer and longer intervals during which they don't need another one.

To explain why results get better with repeated use, Dr. Kane uses this analogy: If you broke your arm playing baseball, you would have to wear a cast for a couple of months. During this time, the muscles would be inactive and would therefore weaken. Once the cast is taken off, the muscles would take a while to return to the same strength as before the arm was broken. The same is true for the muscles paralyzed from a Botox injection. Botox paralyzes the facial muscles and therefore when Botox wears off, the muscles are weakened from inactivity. Now, let's suppose that the cast is put back on the arm shortly after it was taken off. The muscles would get weak once again, but these muscles started off much weaker than the first time the cast was put on. This is similar to what happens with repeated Botox injections. With repeated injections, there is long-term weakening of muscles,

COSMETIC SURGERY AS A CAREER

Just as cosmetic drugs are on the rise, so too is the number of doctors practicing cosmetic medicine. Legally, any doctor can perform cosmetic surgery, which makes it easy for doctors to get into the field or add it to their current area of expertise. For example, the International Society of Cosmetogynecology encourages gynecologists to add cosmetic drugs and surgery as an extension of their practice since both fields target women. The organization holds weekend-long classes on liposuction and injectables.

An appealing aspect of cosmetic medicine is that patients pay with cash the day they get their treatment. In this case, doctors generally do not have to deal with insurance. With the high costs of maintaining a medical practice, expanding services to include cosmetic medicine offers doctors a relatively easy way to boost revenue.

meaning that patients will need less-frequent injections to maintain the same result. Although the idea of long-term muscle weakness would make many people uncomfortable, most patients who get Botox treatments love this result since they do not have to return for injections as often.

Although repeated Botox may cause long-term weakening of muscles, there hasn't been a reported case of someone who has permanently lost all muscle control from Botox. Many health practitioners wonder about the long-term effects of Botox on diligent patients. Dr. Kane relates a story in his book, *The Botox Book*, about a loyal patient of his who received years of Botox injections. Upon seeing her more than a year after his last injection, he noticed that there was still good muscle control and asked who had been doing her injections. She responded with surprise and said she would never go to anyone else; the muscle control was due to the injection she received more than a year before. Based on Dr. Kane's experience, patients receiving Botox for 10 years generally need an injection only once every 12 to 18 months.

Scientists at the Scripps Research Institute in La Jolla, California, have discovered a molecule that increases the effectiveness of Botox by superactivating the botulinum neurotoxin. To recap, Botox's success is due to the toxin's ability to attach to the nerve endings that are responsible for telling the muscles to contract. The results last only so long. The molecule that the scientists in La Jolla discovered has been shown in the lab to increase the effectiveness of the toxin fourteenfold, a tremendous increase.

This Botox-enhancing molecule is an **enzyme**. Enzymes are proteins that accelerate a chemical reaction without being consumed in the process. For example, enzymes in the stomach are able to break down food for digestion. Without these digestive enzymes, we would not be able to access many of the vitamins and minerals in our foods. The enzyme that increases Botox's effectiveness attaches to the toxin and enables it to be activated more easily. One advantage to increasing effectiveness is that smaller doses can be used to get a satisfying result, which would reduce the cost of a single treatment.

THE DANGERS OF BOTOX

"The poison is in the dose" is a saying that is true in the case of botulinum toxin A. A small amount of the toxin can improve a health condition, but a large dose can be fatal. Scientists estimate that it would take 3,000 units of Botox injected into a muscle to cause death; a typical Botox injection is 20 to 40 units. And since the toxin is purified, meaning no part of it is alive or able to reproduce, there is no way the toxin can become lethal from the appropriate formulation and amount of Botox, barring unforseen side effects.

In contrast to the relative safety of Botox, the active form botulinum toxin A is one of the world's most potent biological weapons.[10] The reason for this designation is that it can paralyze motor nerves in the diaphragm, which causes a person to stop breathing; this is what happens when someone gets botulism. Since the active toxin also can be isolated and injected, it presents a threat in the hands of those wanting to do harm.

Although much research exists on these toxins, the exact mechanism of the toxin entering the cell is not fully understood. This is significant since antidotes are more easily developed when it is known how the toxin works. An antidote is a medication used to counteract the effect of a poison. Because they do not understand exactly how these toxins paralyze muscles, scientists have not been able to create an antidote for botulinum toxin A. However, scientists from Howard Hughes Medical Institute recently were able to determine more precisely where the toxin enters the cell. Gaining a better understanding of how the toxin works will enable scientists to one day design a protective drug to stop botulinum toxin A's deadly effects before they start to take hold.

Many people fear that Botox could cause permanent facial paralysis, which is not unreasonable considering such conditions do exist. **Bell's palsy** is a condition in which people temporarily lose all control of facial muscles on one side of the face. This is a full paralysis, meaning there is no communication between nerves and muscles, although people often regain strength and movement in these muscles at some point. In some cases, Bell's palsy is brought on by pregnancy and in others it is caused by an infection that disrupts the facial nerves. Stroke victims also can suffer from a visible facial paralysis. When a stroke occurs, the blood supply to the brain is suddenly blocked, which sometimes results in brain damage. The damage to the brain affects the body's ability to control movement and the result is paralysis.

In the case of Botox injections, however, there is never truly a complete paralysis, meaning there is always some degree of activity in the nerves, even if it is only 2 percent of what it was immediately before an injection. This means that a Botox injection does not cause a full paralysis, as seen in Bell's palsy or in stroke patients. Medical professionals are also able to localize the paralysis when giving a Botox injection so that muscles associated with blinking and eating are not affected. The biggest dangers surrounding Botox, then, are incorrect formulations of the drug and human error in administering it.

There have, however, been rare cases of patients having an adverse reaction to Botox. In 2008, the FDA issued a warning about the link between the use of Botox and botulism symptoms. The warning followed 16 cases of people exhibiting botulism symptoms after receiving injections, four of whom died. The majority of these patients were children with cerebral palsy who had been given Botox to relax spastic muscles. It is not known how or why in these rare cases that the toxin spread beyond the injection site, although it is known that people with neuromuscular disorders such as cerebral palsy are more likely to have an adverse reaction to the drug; in addition the Botox doses given to calm the muscle spasms associated with cerebral palsy are larger than the doses intended to smooth wrinkles. The FDA stressed that patients who receive Botox for any reason—medical or cosmetic—should seek immediate care if they experience any symptoms of botulism, including difficulty swallowing or breathing, slurred speech, or muscle weakness.

IMPOSTOR BOTOX

In the fall of 2004, Dr. Eric Kaplan, a South Florida chiropractor and acupuncturist, and his wife, Bonnie, went to a doctor to get Botox injections in the hopes of achieving a younger appearance. Instead, they nearly died, as he described it in his 2006 book *Dying to Be Young: From Botox to Botulism.*

Shortly after receiving shots of what they thought were Botox at a clinic in Oakland Park, Florida, the Kaplans fell ill. At first they had flulike symptoms, but within days they were not able to move, breathe, see, or speak. These are symptoms of botulism. Their doctor, Bach McComb, was of no help to them in determining what could be wrong because he did not want to admit that the injected product was not Botox, but a dangerous imitation formula. The Kaplans were admitted to the hospital in serious condition.

Around the same time, Dr. McComb and his girlfriend became so ill with similar symptoms that they went to the emergency room. Dr. McComb was known as an entrepreneur who instructed doctors in how to cut costs by making their own Botox-like concoctions, as well as collagen. One doctor commented that the advertisements often came through as faxes and that the product's price was suspiciously cheap.

Learning of these events, the Centers for Disease Control and Prevention (CDC) and Florida state health officials investigated. Since Botox has a track record of being safe, it was suspected that Dr. McComb had used a knock-off brand that was dangerous. Unfortunately, Dr. McComb, his girlfriend, and the Kaplans were so ill with what was then confirmed as botulism that they could not provide information to officials. The officials quickly closed the clinic that Dr. McComb used to give the injections, secured documents, and raided the clinic that they believed supplied the toxin.

It soon came to light that at the time he was administering his Botox-like concoctions, Dr. McComb actually had had his medical license suspended for overprescribing painkillers. In fact, Dr. McComb also had previously been arrested in January 2003 on 10 felony counts of trafficking addictive pain medications, including oxycodone, hydrocodone, and methadone.

Paperwork confiscated from Dr. McComb's clinic showed purchases of the botulinum toxin from an Arizona company, Powderz Inc., and its sister company, Toxin Research International. This toxin was intended for research purposes and was labeled "Not for Human Use," meaning that it is illegal to use on people. It was discovered through the investigation that Dr. McComb improperly diluted the powdered toxin, making it 10 times stronger than Botox. The Kaplans had been led to believe that Dr. McComb was a licensed doctor who knew what he was doing and that he was injecting them with Botox and not some cheap alternative. The Kaplans' misplaced trust and their neglect in researching Dr. McComb cost them money, their health—and nearly their lives.

It can take up to a year for paralysis from botulism to subside. Even months after the injections, Bonnie Kaplan had improved only slightly from paralysis, could barely speak, and still required a ventilator, for more than 22 hours a day, to breathe. In the end, Dr. McComb required a walker when he appeared in court to plead guilty to a felony count of misbranding a drug, and he received three years in prison.

Since the product they were injected with was not Botox, this event did not bring into question the safety of Botox. However, cases such as this explain why all consumers should be careful about the drugs they take and which doctors they trust. Question the doctor's credentials and the products and treatments he or she prescribes. Ask a doctor you trust, such as a primary care physician, to recommend a specialist. If in doubt, ask to see the bottle of the product being injected. When it comes to protecting your personal health and safety, only you will have your best interest in mind.

3

Pump up the Volume: Facial Fillers

Donna is in her late 30s and likes the way she looks, for the most part. She doesn't smoke, works out regularly, and maintains a healthy diet. She feels young and resents the deepening lines around her mouth and lessening volume of her face. She's gotten Botox in the past, but now she'd like to add **facial fillers** *to help rejuvenate her look. Based on the changes she wanted to see, her doctor came up with a customized plan: hyaluronic acid to fill lips and creases, collagen for lines in thinner tissues such as around the eyes, poly-L-lactic acid (**PLLA**) to create new curves in the face, and Botox to increase the length of time the fillers stay put. (If muscles aren't tugging on the areas with fillers, the drug will usually last longer.) Each of these treatments can be done in 30 minutes with instantly visible results—with the exception of PLLA, which might need an additional treatment to get the desired result.*

Plastic surgeons now think that volume loss is a more significant factor in the appearance of aged skin, hence the relatively recent focus on products that add volume, such as facial fillers. Facial fillers are drugs that are injected deep within the dermis of skin to add volume and contour. Aged skin is similar to a deflated balloon. There is excess, which could be stretched and pulled, but what it really needs is more volume. In a balloon, volume would come from air, whereas for sagging skin, volume would come from collagen or other facial fillers.

Facial fillers are popular in large part because of how simple the procedure is. Face-lifts, liposuction, and some other cosmetic procedures require hospital stays and subject patients to increased risk. Fillers can be completed in a few easy office visits. Since 1997, the number of nonsurgical cosmetic procedures has increased 726 percent.[11] Of all the nonsurgical cosmetic applications, soft tissue augmentation—the use of facial fillers—is the third most popular procedure, behind Botox and laser hair removal, respectively.

Fillers are often used with other treatments such as Botox. Although fillers have the same general purpose—to add volume—dozens of different kinds of fillers exist based on particle size and how long the product will stay in the face. For example, a filler with less volume—smaller particle size—would be more appropriate for thinner tissues, such as those around the eyes. Large wrinkles would benefit more with fillers of larger particle size. The other factor in choosing the right facial filler is determining how long the filler needs to last. A more permanent filler would seem to be the obvious choice, but sometimes a longer-lasting filler might not look or feel as natural as a less permanent filler because of its consistency and where it is injected into the face. For example, some longer-lasting particle fillers can cause a person to develop **granulomas**, which are tiny bumps that can be felt, and sometimes seen, under the skin. Only a well-qualified doctor should make decisions about which filler to use or the results could look unbalanced.

One added benefit of fillers is their ability to stimulate collagen production. Scientists first suspected this when they noticed that people getting repeated treatments seemed to need less frequent injections. The process of stimulating collagen production is known as **neocollagenesis**. In a younger person, the protein cells that make collagen, which are located in the dermis, are naturally stretched in a way that encourages new collagen production. When older skin sags, these cells are no longer stretched, so collagen production decreases.

Figure 3.1 Here is a color scanning electron micrograph (SEM) of a healthy collagen fiber. Collagen is the most abundant protein in the body, and can be found in the bones, tendons, and body tissues. *(© BSIP / Photo Researchers, Inc.)*

The filler stretches the protein cells in the dermis that make collagen, in a sense, just as when the skin was younger. This stretching stimulates production of more collagen.

An important aspect of all injectable fillers is that the results are not permanent because the body will metabolize the product in the filler. It's also hard to predict how long the filler will last, since it depends on factors such as an individual's skin quality and lifestyle. If a filler is injected into an area where there is a lot of muscle movement, it is likely not to last as long as an injection in a less active site. In an effort to offset absorption, doctors will often "overfill" a site—that is, inject slightly more than the desired amount to compensate for immediate absorption. As a result, patients usually appear slightly puffier than desired following treatment but the cosmetic improvements last longer.

FAT AS A FILLER

Using a patient's own body fat as a facial filler is another way to reduce the appearance of wrinkles. The process, which takes anywhere from 15 minutes to an hour, begins when the doctor removes fat from the patient's abdomen. The doctor is then able to purify the fat in a quickly moving device called a centrifuge. The doctor then puts this pure fat into a large syringe for injection deep within the layers of skin.

The advantage of using a patient's fat versus other skin fillers is that there is very little chance of an allergic reaction since the fat is coming from the person's own body. Also, greater volumes of fat can be used as compared to other fillers so it can be used to fill deeper wrinkles and contours. However, injecting larger amounts of fat can cause swelling that lasts several days to several weeks; for a patient who wants to return to work right after the treatment, using a smaller amount of fat is recommended.

Patients can expect to see a reduction in wrinkles and sagging as a result of the filler. As with most cosmetic drugs, the results are not permanent. This is because the body will reabsorb about half of the fat injected within six months after the treatment. This reabsorbtion of fat does not harm the body. Since this treatment is not permanent, patients have to repeat treatments to continue to have a more youthful appearance.

COLLAGEN

Collagen is a protein that occurs naturally in the body. It adds elasticity and volume to skin. Our bodies produce less of it as we age, resulting in wrinkles and folds. Collagen is a popular filler for the skin around the nose, mouth, and lips. Collagen used for injections is often **bovine-based**, meaning it is derived from cows, and it is formulated in varying thicknesses depending on the patient's needs (brand names include Zyderm and Zyplast). Collagen from humans is also used as a filler (brand names include CosmoDerm and CosmoPlast). The FDA first approved collagen for use as a filler in 1981.

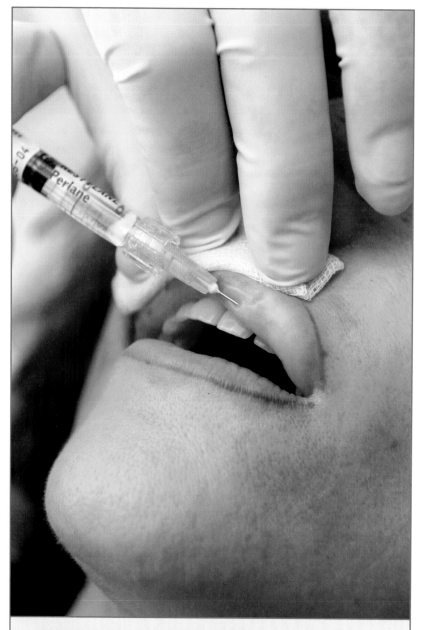

Figure 3.2   This woman is having collagen injected into her upper lip. (© CC Studio / Photo Researchers, Inc)

Since collagen is not extracted from the patient's body, it presents a greater risk of allergic reaction than fat injections. Some doctors will perform an allergy test a month before the injection. After it is determined that the patient is not allergic to collagen, the filler can be injected with a needle in a relatively quick procedure—usually in the doctor's office. Mild swelling may occur from the injection. After this swelling has subsided, the skin should appear more smooth and taut.

HYALURONIC ACID

In 2000, ABC News sent Connie Chung to Yuzuri Hara, a small Japanese village that was nicknamed the Village of Long Life because of the youthfulness of its residents. The village residents consumed a healthy diet of local root vegetables and sticky starches, such as sweet potatoes. It is widely believed in the country that they have a younger appearance and live longer lives. This village did not have one case of skin cancer and 10 percent of the residents were more than 85 years old. A Japanese pharmaceutical company did some research and discovered that the villagers' diet stimulated production of hyaluronic acid (HA), leading the company to develop HA pills.

HA, also known as hyaluronan or glycosaminoglycan, was first used in the 1940s as an egg white substitute. This long-chained sugar molecule is referred to as a "goo" molecule because of its consistency. It occurs naturally in skin and cartilage and connects water to the body's tissues. The body needs moisture to maintain its systems and HA helps maintain these moisture levels. HA works by "floating" skin cells to add volume and structure. It also prevents the breakdown of collagen. As we age, the body produces less HA, which contributes to wrinkling as well as joint ailments since HA also acts as a lubricant to joints.

HA has become an increasingly popular agent for soft tissue augmentation. HA is the main ingredient in Restylane, the most widely used dermal filler in North America.[12] (Other brand names using HA include Hylaform and Juvéderm.) Restylane is used to smooth wrinkles and acne scars, to volumize lips, and to add volume to the backs of hands. HA products are also used for brow lifts. The risk of having an allergic reaction to HA is low, probably because it occurs naturally in the skin. Because of this, HA does not have to be tested on the skin before a treatment, so patients can make one less trip to the doctor's office. Results are usually immediate and slightly longer lasting than with other fillers (6 to 12 months), although the filler is eventually absorbed into the body. Another reason that HA is popular is its flexibility—it can be adjusted in terms of thickness depending on whether a deep groove or a fine line is being filled.

POLY-L-LACTIC ACID (PLLA)

PLLA is a biodegradable, semipermanent filler and an **alpha hydroxy acid** that is used to treat a significant loss of facial volume. It is primarily used for HIV-related loss of facial fat under the trade name Sculptra. Those with HIV suffer more significant loss of facial fat than do people going through the aging process. Like other fillers, PLLA boosts the body's natural collagen production. PLLA is commonly used off-label for cosmetic purposes, such as lessening pronounced nasolabial folds and rejuvenating the back of hands. A couple of treatments are usually required to see a satisfying result, which can last up to two years.

Because the results are longer lasting than with other fillers, health practitioners must be much more careful about application, since an unwanted result causes a more significant problem. Lopsidedness can occur if the doctor does not properly shake the vial before injecting half of the vial on each side of the face. It can be corrected with another injection to the side of the face that is less full.

After PLLA is injected, the face must be vigorously massaged to distribute and sculpt the filler into place. PLLA does not occur naturally in the body, but it is absorbed into the body over the two- to three-year period after injection and breaks down into lactic acid, which does occur naturally in the body. The lactic acid is then absorbed harmlessly into the body, according to the manufacturer.

A NONSURGICAL "FACE-LIFT"

Women today are replacing surgical face-lifts with a "liquid face-lift" by using a combination of dermal fillers. The cosmetic drug industry is responding by providing an increasing array of fillers of varying particle sizes depending on the depth of fill needed. Another significant variable is how long the filler lasts; consumers want longer-lasting results but with a fine balance of still looking natural and not "plastic."

4

Topical Wrinkle Reducers and Cellulite Treatments

Topical treatments are applied to the surface of the skin, usually in the form of a lotion or other solution. Topical treatments are easier to use than injections but are limited in the skin ailments they can treat. The effectiveness of topical treatments depends on how deeply the drug needs to penetrate the skin.

Topical treatments can work well for mild acne since the product can improve skin by simply penetrating the epidermis to unclog pores. If the product is needed to treat a skin condition that originates in the subcutaneous layer, such as cellulite, it is much less likely to be effective. Topical treatments such as chemical peels are also quite effective because the drug has to penetrate only the epidermis to rejuvenate skin cell production.

RETINOIDS (RETINOL) OR TRETINOIN

Retinoids are chemically similar to vitamin A. Products with retinoid or retinol in them claim to minimize lines and wrinkles associated with sun damage. Originally, retinoids were used to treat acne, but then older patients using them discovered an improvement in their skin's texture, specifically a reduction in fine lines. Retinoids work by stimulating new growth of tiny blood vessels; this helps regenerate skin cells. Retinoids also stimulate the collagen and elastic fibers in the skin. Finally, these products halt **free radicals**, which weaken and damage skin cells, leading to collagen breakdown, a decrease in elasticity, and wrinkling.

HYDROXY ACIDS AND CHEMICAL PEELS

Hydroxy acids encourage **exfoliation**. Exfoliation is the process of removing old cells to encourage the growth of new cells. Hydroxy acids slough off dead cells on the outermost layer of the skin, thus stimulating the skin to grow newer cells. Ideally, the new skin will be thicker and have a smoother, more rejuvenated appearance. Hydroxy acids include alpha hydroxy acids (AHAs) and beta hydroxy acids (BHAs). AHAs and BHAs are

ANTIOXIDANTS AND FREE RADICALS

Antioxidants are chemicals believed to protect and repair the skin by boosting collagen production. They also strengthen blood vessels. Common antioxidants are vitamins A, C, E, and beta-carotene. Antioxidants disable destructive molecules referred to as free radicals. Causes of free radicals include air pollution, sunlight, alcohol, and cigarette smoke.[13] Over one's lifetime it would be nearly impossible to avoid free radical damage, the cumulative effect of which is believed to be one of the causes of skin aging.

Given this, it's easy to understand why many products would boast of an antioxidant component. Antioxidants can be ingested as well as applied to the skin. One option is to eat foods containing these vitamins, such as fruits. Antioxidants are also available in a pill version, often at levels much higher than the recommended daily dose. More is not necessarily better, though; higher amounts of these antioxidants have not been found to be better than the recommended doses, according to some researchers. Studies on whether antioxidants can slow aging have shown varying results. The best strategy to fight free radical damage is to eat a healthy diet with lots of fruits and vegetables that naturally contain antioxidants.

found in nature—for example, in fruit. The chemical structures and modes of action differ.

Alpha Hydroxy Acids

AHAs became popular in skin care creams during the mid-1990s. The most commonly used AHA is glycolic acid, which comes from sugarcane and sugar beets. In 1997, the FDA expressed concern about the safety of AHAs based on a study sponsored by the cosmetics industry, which showed that use of AHAs increases the skin's sun sensitivity. Although the study clearly showed that people using AHAs had sun sensitivity while using these products, it is not known exactly why AHAs cause skin sensitivity.

AHAs must be absorbed into the skin to take effect; therefore, creams that are applied are recommended and cleansers that are washed off are not. The extent of exfoliation from AHAs varies with the concentration and the acidity of the specific AHAs being used. A product with AHAs will list some of the following ingredients on its label:

- glycolic acid
- lactic acid
- malic acid
- citric acid
- glycolic acid + ammonium glycolate
- alpha-hydroxyethanoic acid
- hydroxycaprylic acid
- mixed fruit acid
- tri-alpha hydroxy fruit acids
- sugarcane extract
- alpha hydroxy and botanical complex
- L-alpha hydroxy acid

Although AHA products do not have to prove scientifically that they improve skin, they are legally required to list their ingredients on the label. Unfortunately, they are not required to state the percentage concentration. In 1997, the FDA received approximately 100 complaints from consumers about AHAs in relation to sun sensitivity. People differ in their abilities to handle different chemicals on their face. The more acidic the product, the greater the chance that it could irritate living skin tissue; on the other hand, a product that is not acidic enough may not be effective. According to Heather Brannon, M.D., AHAs work best in a concentration of 5 to 8 percent, which would mean the acid would be listed second or third on the list of ingredients.[14]

AHAs are also used in most chemical peels. Chemical peels are meant to correct sun damage, reduce mild scarring, reduce the appearance of wrinkles, remove stubborn blackheads, improve dark skin discoloration, and temporarily reduce excessive skin oils. AHA peels consist of glycolic, lactic, or fruit acids, which are usually gentler on the skin. The AHAs used in peels tend to have a lower pH level (higher acidity) and a higher concentration level than most over-the-counter cosmetics. Over-the-counter AHA products must have a concentration level of less than 10 percent. A glycolic acid chemical peel, however, has a concentration level of 70 to 99 percent glycolic acid compound and must be purchased and applied by a health care practitioner.

The higher the percent of acid, the longer lasting the results will be. However, the more acidic the peel is, the more likely there will be flaking, severe redness, and oozing that could last for up to four weeks. Obviously, people who suffer from burning or redness with AHA products should not consider chemical peels.

Beta Hydroxy Acids

Beta hydroxy acid (BHA) is salicylic acid. Salicylic acid has been used to treat acne for decades. This acid occurs naturally in wintergreen leaves and the bark of some trees. The main difference between AHAs and BHAs is that AHAs are water-soluble and BHAs are oil-soluble. As a result, BHAs generally penetrate more deeply into the skin and can penetrate oily areas to remove blackheads that are in oily pores. BHAs also help to reduce the appearance of fine lines and wrinkles. Like AHAs, they encourage more rapid cell turnover, and thus they should be used in combination with sun protection. BHAs are better suited for people with oily skin, whereas AHAs are better for thickened, sun-damaged skin where acne is not an issue. Products with BHAs may list the following ingredients on their labels:

- salicylic acid

- willow extract

- salicylate

- beta hydroxybutanoic acid

- trophic acid

- trethocanic acid

Beta hydroxy acids can also be used for chemical peels. These peels use 20 to 30 percent salicylic acid. They lift the topmost layer of skin by dissolving cell structures that bind it to the epidermis. The result is a jolt of new cell division and the shedding of old cells, enhancing the effect of over-the-counter BHAs. Chemical peels using salicylic acid are generally more intense than glycolic peels. People who scar easily should not do a salicylic acid peel, or a strong chemical peel of any kind. Sun protection after a peel is crucial because the sun's ultraviolet rays will more easily damage the new cells. It is important to remember that a chemical peel can improve the appearance of the skin but will not slow the aging process.

TCA Peels

Another chemical peel is a so-called blue peel that is a mix of trichloroacetic acid (TCA) and glycine. This peel turns blue when it has been on the face just the right length of time. With this treatment the improvement to the skin takes time to reveal itself: The skin looks worse—much worse—before it looks better. Many people schedule this type of peel around a vacation so that they can hide out while they are healing.

In this process, a technician at a skin clinic covers the face with a liquid, which takes about 10 minutes to turn blue. Patients leave the clinic with pills to reduce itching and instructions not to touch their face because germs from their hands could cause an infection on the new raw skin. The next day the skin usually appears shiny with no signs of peeling, but by the second day the skin appears brownish and the lines deeper than prior to the treatment. By day four, the skin is dry, cracked, and brown. Five days posttreatment, new skin begins to appear while the old skin continues to peel off in strips.

The objective of this peel is to generate new, better skin by causing the old skin to peel off. It usually takes a couple of months to see a big difference. Many people report that although the treatment was uncomfortable, they would likely go through it again because of the final results.

A TCA peel is stronger than an AHA peel. A TCA peel gives a medium-depth peel and is used to treat superficial blemishes, pigment problems, and surface wrinkles. A full-face peel can be accomplished in 15 minutes. Mild TCA peels can be repeated monthly, but stronger ones should be repeated only every six months or annually depending on skin sensitivity.

Phenol Peels

A phenol peel is the strongest, deepest type of skin peel. A phenol peel is used by people who have coarse wrinkles or even precancerous growths. It generally takes 7 to 10 days for new skin to grow after a phenol peel. In the meantime, the face will

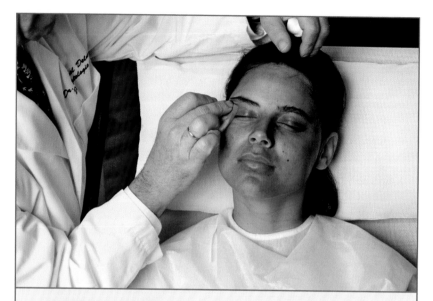

Figure 4.1 Trichloroacetic acid (TCA) peels are used to treat brown spots and superficial wrinkles. *(© VOISIN/PHANIE / Photo Researchers, Inc.)*

appear red. Pain medication may even be prescribed during this period. Unlike with a TCA peel, after a phenol peel the skin will still be able to produce pigment (i.e., tan). A phenol peel may permanently remove freckles since the pigment associated with freckles is at a shallow skin depth. Sometimes retinol is used prior to a TCA or phenol chemical peel. The retinol medication thins out the skin's surface layer, allowing the chemical peel solution to be absorbed more evenly and deeply.

The use of very deep TCA peels (those that require two weeks of recuperation) has been examined more closely for its use in removing precancerous skin growths. A study in the *Archives of Dermatology* compared the results of three treatments for precancerous skin lesions: TCA peels, a topical cream, and carbon dioxide resurfacing. All treatments helped reduce the number of lesions, but those using the TCA peel saw a fortyfold reduction in skin cancer.[15]

CHEMICAL PEELS AND THE HAYFLICK LIMIT

There is little dispute that all of these acid-based products (AHAs, BHAs, TCAs, and phenols) encourage cell rejuvenation. The question is whether skin cells can divide indefinitely without "catching" on to the stimuli of these products. If not, patients might see a less significant result as they continue to use these products. According to the International Rosacea Foundation, certain cells in the skin will divide 50 times and then enter a period of senescence, or dormancy, meaning that they will no longer divide. This limit of 50 cell divisions is referred to as the Hayflick limit. At the Hayflick limit, skin cells will no longer respond to signals to divide. Skin with many senescent cells looks like the opposite of newly rejuvenated skin: It's often blotchy and wrinkled or more easily wrinkled. In some situations, however, such as with cancer cells, skin cells will not limit their number of divisions. The Hayflick limit exists, it's believed, as the body's natural defense to prevent cancer.

CELLULITE TREATMENTS

Cellulite is a type of body fat known for giving skin a dimply appearance. It tends to appear as people age, when the fat cells begin to protrude through weakened, less elastic layers of the dermis. Women are more likely to have cellulite than men because women generally have a higher percentage of body fat. In fact, nearly all women will develop cellulite on their bodies at some point in their lives. According to the International Society of Cosmetogynecology, more than 90 percent of women have some cellulite, although the severity can range from mild dimpling to significant bulging referred to as the "mattress" phenomenon.

At one time, when food was not as plentiful as it is today, the appearance of cellulite was considered a symbol of beauty and wealth. Today, many Western cultures dictate that cellulite is unsightly and many companies have developed products to meet the demands of consumers desiring to reduce its appearance. Most of these products are in the form of creams, although injection procedures have also been developed.

Cellulite Creams

Some products describe cellulite as fat that is trapped that needs circulation, and that cellulite develops in areas where circulation has decreased. The analogy of cellulite as "trapped fat" is a fair one in that the fat has protruded through a layer of skin in the subcutaneous tissue and will not naturally go back.[16] Due to this understanding of cellulite, many of the cellulite products claim to increase circulation to "release" the fat.

According to BodyandFitness.com, which promotes cellulite cream on its Web site, cellulite is trapped in the natural honeycomb fibers under our skin, and the tissues surrounding the fat are weakened, leaking toxins. The Web site claims that a blend of herbs can increase blood flow and metabolism, thus freeing the fat. The herbs it recommends include dandelion, red clover, and cayenne. Other cellulite creams include extracts of black pepper seed, sweet orange peel, gingerroot, cinnamon bark, green tea, and caffeine.

Aminophylline is another common ingredient in many cellulite creams. Aminophylline is a prescription drug that opens lung passageways, also known as a **bronchodilator**. It is prescribed to people who have shortness of breath, asthma, chronic bronchitis, and other lung diseases. BodyandFitness. com claims that studies have shown that women who use a skin cream containing aminophylline lose inches of fat from their body in a matter of weeks. The explanation is that, like the herbs mentioned above, aminophylline stimulates blood flow and circulation so that the cellulite can be burned and flushed out of the body.

Claims that creams improve circulation and are a cure for cellulite are on unsteady scientific grounds. Studies conflict as to whether any of these products actually achieve any results. One study, published in *Obesity Research* in 1995, declared that

Figure 4.2 There are many creams on the market that claim to diminish the appearance of cellulite. *(© James Keyser/Time & Life Pictures/Getty Images)*

aminophylline was effective. Many creams soon began adding this product and claiming to reduce cellulite. Not all scientific studies are created equal, though. It was later discovered that one of the researchers on the *Obesity Research* study was involved in the marketing of an aminophylline cream.

Retinol and alpha hydroxy acids (AHAs) are other active ingredients in creams promoted to treat cellulite. Retinol and AHAs work on the skin, improving skin texture. Since the appearance of cellulite is exacerbated by aging, inelastic skin, these drugs could have merit, in theory, although the improvement would likely be slight.

Mesotherapy

Mesotherapy is another approach to controlling cellulite. It involves injecting a concoction—typically containing vitamins, enzymes, and minerals—into the fat under the skin. The small doses are administered with tiny needles in the areas of the body with cellulite. Like cellulite creams, the injection from mesotherapy is supposed to interact with fat cells, enabling them to release fat to be burned as energy or reducing their size, which decreases the puckering of the skin.

The International Society of Cosmetogynecology, which supports mesotherapy, recommends 10 to 15 sessions for mesotherapy to correct the appearance of cellulite; each session generally ranges from $300 to $450. Unlike treatments such as liposuction, mesotherapy does not rid the body of the entire fat cell, just the fat in the cell. This means that a patient could see a lessening of cellulite but later have a "rebound" problem if she gains weight, because the amount of fat in the cells would increase. No scientific studies confirming the success of mesotherapy have been published, and the medical community is skeptical of mesotherapy's effectiveness.

THE CLAIMS OF COSMETIC DRUGS: FACT VERSUS FICTION

The makers of cosmetic drugs are not always required to give scientific proof to support their claims. However, the FDA has intervened on many occasions to prohibit flagrant abuse of labeling laws.

Some of these cases have involved fraudulent claims by makers of cellulite treatments and weight-loss cures. In 1991, Slender You, Inc., was pursued by the FDA for claiming that its tablets enabled people to lose weight, firm muscles, and remove cellulite, among other things. The product was referred to as "continuous passive motion tablets," indicating that the benefits of activity were achieved through the tablets even with no movement. There was no scientific basis for this claim. The company signed a consent and discontinued their false claims.[17]

Another noteworthy cellulite claim crackdown occurred in Iowa in 1999. New York City-based Lipo Slim, Inc., was promoting Lipo Slim Briefs in Iowa. The ads claimed that the underpants would "get rid of your cellulite" and "dissolve fat and deposits that accumulate in hips, stomachs, buttocks, and thighs." One ad by the company, placed in the *National Enquirer*, said "thousands of thermo-active micropore cells" in the briefs created a massage that destroyed fat. The claims were all without any scientific proof. The Iowa attorney general required the company to offer full refunds to all customers ($19.95 to $29.95, depending on the size) in Iowa and pay $12,000 to the state consumer education fund. Any future advertising the company did had to specify that the product was not available in Iowa.[18]

GOING DEEPER: LIPODISSOLVE

Lipodissolve is a treatment similar to mesotherapy. The difference is that the injections are deeper and the drug— referred to as PCDC—is approved in Germany but not the U.S. PCDC, short for phosphatidylcholine deoxycholate, is an enzyme derived from the soybean that breaks down fatty deposits. Whereas mesotherapy is meant more for cellulite, lipodissolve can be used to treat fat layers anywhere. The end result is meant to be the same, though: The fat, often in the abdomen and buttocks on women, and in "love handles" on men, breaks down and melts away.

Lipodissolve has little science to back up any claims that it works, and the medical community is skeptical. The lipodissolve procedure, as well as the drug injected during this procedure, is not approved by the FDA. There are also concerns that dissolving the fat in the body could aggravate heart conditions. Until science can convince consumers that this procedure does not work, there will likely continue to be patients willing to spend thousands of dollars in the hopes that their fat can be dissolved.

The above cases serve as an important reminder that while a product promoted as a "cure" might be popular, its effects may still be unproven. Unbiased medical studies must be done to ensure that a product does what it claims to do and is safe to use. A scientific experiment from which conclusions can be drawn must adhere to certain study designs and must be repeatable. In addition, it's important to note who is funding the study. Be wary if a claim cites research that supposedly proves the product works and the company funded its own research. Valid research by scientists is generally presented at annual meetings and published in a journal reviewed by scientists in the same field, such as dermatology. Fashion magazines may contain ads that make medical claims that are not reviewed by scientists and therefore are not necessarily a good resource for whether a product works based on proven science.

5

Treatments for Hair Loss

Nick is a 31-year-old Philadelphia attorney and probably one of the last men you'd expect to spend a considerable amount of money on cosmetic drugs. As the youngest of seven, with all of his older brothers completely bald by the age of 30, he turned to Propecia, a drug that prevents baldness. The active ingredient in Propecia is **finasteride**, *which prevents baldness by inhibiting an enzyme. The drug works only if he uses it consistently, and his insurance does not reimburse him for this cosmetic drug. He's so committed to maintaining his current hairline that he's more likely to fall behind on loan repayments for law school than not buy his hair medications!*

HALTING HAIR LOSS

Men represent an increasing share of the cosmetic market. Antiaging creams are becoming more popular among them, with companies such as L'Oreal creating product lines aimed at men. Manufacturers believe the increasing popularity is due to not only a desire to look good but also to concerns about skin cancer. An even greater concern for many men is treating hair loss.

Each year, American men spend more than a billion dollars on drugs, surgical procedures, and hairpieces to fight baldness. Drugs to fight baldness are outpacing the alternatives because the outcome is authentic and it is easy to take a pill. The catches are that the patient must take the medication early on to stave off hair loss and that it must be used continually to keep further hair loss at bay.

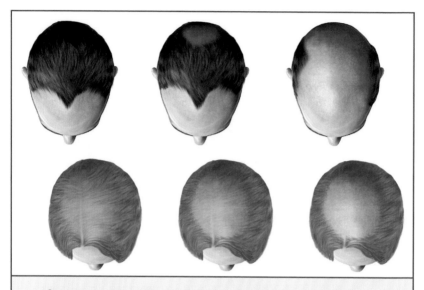

Figure 5.1 These illustrations show the typical progression of baldness in men *(top)* and, more rarely, in women *(bottom)*. (© *Nucleus Medical Art / Visuals Unlimited*)

To understand why it is so vital to use antibaldness drugs consistently, it's important to understand the relationship between hair and hormones. Hair grows from hair follicles. Follicles are the oblong structures within the skin that protect and mold the hair shaft. The follicle also contains a tiny muscle at the bottom that is responsible for making hair stand erect. Hair is composed of dead protein cells called keratin, whereas the follicle is made up of live cells. Hair follicles are formed very early in life—before we are even born. After birth, no more follicles are formed on the body.

Genetics, age, and testosterone levels are the main factors that determine whether someone will go bald. Nick is correct for fearing that he will become bald since all the men in his family are bald. Scientists now believe they have isolated the gene that causes baldness. The gene, referred to as LIPH, is defective in those with baldness. The LIPH creates an enzyme called **dihydrotestosterone (DHT)**. When this enzyme comes into contact with the testosterone in the hair follicle, it creates a byproduct that dries up the hair follicle. Wherever DHT is present in the hair follicle, the hair dries up, causing the hair to grow shorter and thinner than areas without DHT. Eventually the hair follicle becomes dormant and hair ceases to grow at all. This scenario occurs in 25 percent of males by age 30, and 66 percent of men will have a balding pattern by age 60, according to the U.S. National Institutes of Health.

The loss of hair for men can be quite devastating. A study by Denison University found that both women and men view bald men as "less physically attractive, less socially skilled, and less socially successful" than their counterparts. [19] Because of these beliefs, cosmetic drugs have been developed to control hair loss. A couple have been approved by the FDA.

CREAMS AND PILLS

Like so many cosmetic drugs, two of the most successful drugs intended for the prevention of hair loss were discovered in the process of treating other ailments. Minoxidil was originally used to treat high blood pressure. While performing experiments on people in 1971, researchers noticed that patients were growing hair on their shoulders, legs, head, and other areas of the body. The researchers then decided to apply some of the product on their arms to see if hair growth increased. After several months, there was a noticeable increase in hair growth. It took until 1988 for Upjohn, the makers of minoxidil, to receive permission from the FDA to sell the drug, which they named Rogaine, as a prescription treatment for hair loss. Researchers still do not understand exactly how minoxidil encourages hair growth. (Minoxidil is still used to treat high blood pressure but under a different trade name, Loniten.)

Minoxidil is applied as a cream or foam and grows hair, reduces hair loss, sustains hair growth, and thickens hair fibers. Unfortunately, it does not work for everyone and often takes a few months to produce results when it does work. Many people get frustrated by how long it takes to see results and switch to other remedies. It must be used consistently to be effective.

Finasteride (Propecia), another approved drug, is taken as a pill. It is chemically similar to steroids and is prescribed strictly for adult men because if used by women it can cause birth defects in her children, if the woman were to become pregnant while taking the drug. Finasteride's ability to control hair loss was discovered by accident during clinical trials for the treatment of enlarged prostate. Propecia works by inhibiting an enzyme that converts testosterone to DHT. DHT is responsible for drying up the hair follicle, eventually stopping hair growth. When finasteride inhibits this conversion from testosterone to DHT, the process of hair loss ceases. Propecia can be quite costly, at approximately $70 a month, and it also requires a prescription.

Propecia is successful for 65 percent of men, according to Merck, the makers of Propecia. Changes don't happen overnight though. In three months, Merck states, patients may see decreased hair loss. It will probably take six months to see new hair growth. After a year of use (and more than $800 in drug costs), patients can determine with certainty if Propecia works for them. After five years of treatment, patients would see the most retention and regrowth they will likely see with Propecia. If they stop taking the medication, however, they will begin losing hair again. Side effects of the drug are minimal, with about 2 percent of patients experiencing breast tenderness and/or enlargement or decreased sex drive.

EMERGING TECHNOLOGY: WNT PROTEINS

Research from the University of Pennsylvania is challenging the accepted idea that hair follicles can't be created. In lab tests, mice were found to grow new follicles on skin that was healing from wounds. The scientists found that certain proteins, called **wnts**, were able to create new follicles.

Wnt proteins come from a family of signaling molecules that regulate interactions between cells during the embryonic

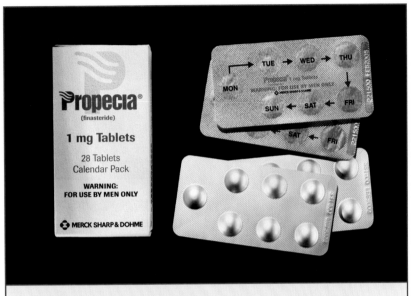

Figure 5.2 Propecia (finasteride) blocks the formation of the hormone dihydrotestosterone (DHT), which is thought to cause hair loss in men. This drug has been shown to slow or even halt the progress of male pattern baldness. *(© Colin Cuthbert / Photo Researchers, Inc.)*

stage of development. They bind to receptors on the cell's surface. These proteins do not necessarily create new follicles when skin is perfectly healed. Wounded skin, however, is receptive to receiving instructions from the proteins. When healing, skin is, in a sense, similar to tissue at the embryonic stage, when new follicles are created.

Theoretically, wnt proteins could be used to grow hair on patients lacking follicles. In those who suffer from baldness, however, a product such as finasteride would still need to be taken to inhibit the enzyme that converts testosterone. If not, the DHT would continue to dry up any new hair from newly developed hair follicles. Cosmetic drugs are often used in combination with other products. Research in this area is still in the early stages.

6

Treatments for Acne and Rosacea

Mark was never the type of teenager to give much thought to his skin, but lately it seems all he can think about. In the past, pimples were an occasional annoyance, but now they cover his entire forehead, chin, and cheeks. He started scrubbing with soap every night but it only reduced the oily appearance and did little to control the painful outbreaks. The blemishes were so large that they felt like large bumps deep within the skin. Mark has cystic acne, which is the type most likely to scar. Cases of cystic acne generally require a dermatologist's care and a couple of treatment approaches.

ACNE

Severe cases of either acne or rosacea can affect a patient's self-esteem and at worst leave significant scarring. Given the effect skin diseases have on people, it comes as no surprise that there are numerous treatment options for these conditions.

Acne can form when abnormal flaking of skin cells occurs within the hair follicle, which then causes the skin cells to clump together. This blockage can become enlarged and even rupture the hair follicle. Hair follicles contain **sebum**, a type of oil that exacerbates the swelling and inflammation. *Propionibacterium acnes* (P. acnes), a bacterium that lives on the skin surface, also can cause acne. *P. acnes* feeds on sebum; it does this by using enzymes that digest the facial oil, which can then redden and irritate the skin.

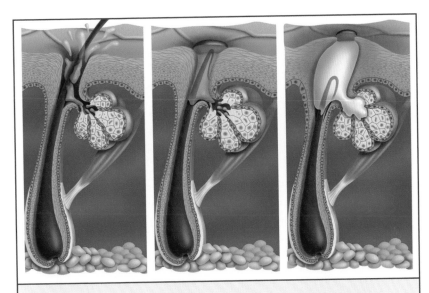

Figure 6.1 These illustrations show how acne forms. The hair that grows from the hair shaft is protected and waterproofed by sebum (oil) from the sebaceous gland *(left)*. If the hair shaft becomes blocked *(center)*, then sebum builds up in the hair shaft. This leads to a pimple, or whitehead *(right)*. *(© Sophie Jacopin / Photo Researchers, Inc.)*

Acne falls into two categories: noninflammatory and inflammatory. Blackheads are one kind of noninflammatory acne. Blackheads form when a pore becomes clogged with cells but is open to the air; the oil inside the pore is the cause for the black appearance. A whitehead can be either noninflammatory or inflammatory and has a similar process to the blackhead, but it is not exposed to the air and may appear pink or white. Inflammatory acne is generally more painful because it causes the skin to become inflamed and red. Inflammatory acne includes pimples and larger, deeper lesions. The most severe form of inflammatory acne is nodular acne, also known as cystic acne. This type of acne is easily identified by pressing down on the blemish; if a bump can be felt deep below the skin, this is a nodule. A nodule is an acne lesion, or cyst, below the skin surface that has become inflamed and ruptured. Nodular or cystic acne will require more than topical treatments to cure.

THE ROLE OF HORMONES IN ACNE

Hormonal fluctuations can influence acne, which is why it is common among adolescents. Acne is not restricted to teenagers, however, and is commonly experienced by adult women in response to hormonal changes. The hormones most responsible for causing acne are **androgens.** Androgens enlarge sebaceous (oil-producing) glands that further clog the hair follicles. During puberty, androgen levels increase, leading to acne in many teenagers.

Estrogen, on the other hand, is a hormone that actually improves acne by reducing the amount of sebum produced by the skin. A woman's estrogen level fluctuates based on factors such as her menstrual cycle, pregnancy, and menopause. As estrogen increases, a woman experiences less acne. When estrogen levels dip, such as during the few days before menstruation, acne can temporarily get worse. Because birth control pills contain estrogen, their manufacturers may advertise an added benefit of acne control.

ACNE TREATMENTS

Acne is common and can be difficult to cure, but a variety of products are available: over-the-counter and prescription, oral and topical. For a moderate to severe case of acne, a dermatologist will likely blend a couple of medications to get the best result.

Salicylic Acid

Salicylic acid is one of the most common ingredients in over-the-counter acne medications. As described in the previous chapter, it speeds cell turnover on the skin surface, minimizing fine lines when used as a chemical peel. In the case of acne treatment, salicylic acid reduces clogging of cells in the hair follicle by minimizing the shedding of cells within the follicle.

Benzoyl Peroxide

Benzoyl peroxide is a topical application that works by killing *P. acnes*. It is the active ingredient in many over-the-counter acne medications. While benzoyl peroxide can dry up existing pimples, it can also cause dryness or redness and irritation in more sensitive skin. Skin often develops a tolerance, however, so these side effects may lessen over time.

Benzoyl peroxide is available in concentrations from 2.5 to 10 percent. Higher concentrations require a prescription. A higher strength is usually more effective but more likely to cause irritation and dryness. Patients with more severe acne may choose to use a higher concentration with the hope that their skin will become tolerant to the medication.

Most dermatologists recommend combining treatments to get the best control over acne. Since salicylic acid and benzoyl peroxide control acne in different ways, a combination of the products is likely to have better results than either product alone.

Retinoids

Retinoids are used both topically and orally to control acne and require a prescription. As mentioned in the previous chapter, this derivative of vitamin A also works to diminish fine lines and wrinkles. In the treatment of acne retinoids work by unclogging pores and preventing whiteheads and blackheads. The biggest drawback to retinoids is their potential to irritate the skin, particularly if the product is excessively applied. Only a small amount should be evenly applied to acne-affected areas. Since increased sun sensitivity is a side effect, it is recommended that patients using retinoids also slather on a high SPF sunblock when spending time outdoors.

Antibiotics

Antibiotics can be used both orally and topically. Oral antibiotics control acne by killing *P. acnes*, which subsequently decreases the inflammation associated with pimples. They are usually meant for moderate to severe acne and often need to be taken regularly for months to see long-lasting results.

Erythromycin is an antibiotic that comes in both topical and oral form. It kills a broad range of bacteria, including *P. acnes*. Clindamycin is another topical antibiotic that controls acne by targeting *P. acnes*. Clindamycin also decreases inflammation. Skin dryness and irritation are possible side effects of these topical antibiotics. If a patient's skin can tolerate topical antibiotics, the use of two products such as erthyromycin and benzoyl peroxide can be more beneficial than one product alone.

The problem with a broad-spectrum antibiotic such as erythromycin, is that some "good" bacteria could be killed along with the disease-causing, or in this case acne-causing, bacteria. Tetracyclines are another group of antibiotics, taken orally, that helps treat the inflammatory lesions of acne. The side effects include staining of the teeth and increased sensitivity to sunlight.

One disadvantage of taking antibiotics to treat acne, or any disease, is that bacteria can eventually become resistant, meaning the drug no longer can kill them. If **microbial resistance** occurs, a different antibiotic would have to be used to control the bacteria.

ROSACEA

Around 14 million Americans, most between the ages of 30 and 60, suffer from a condition called rosacea. Rosacea is a chronic inflammation of the skin, usually affecting the face but sometimes other parts of the body. As recently as 1992, rosacea was considered a rare disease and only one FDA-approved drug was available for treating it. This drug was referred to as an **orphan drug**. At the time, the FDA believed that a mere 200,000 Americans suffered from this condition, when in fact most people with rosacea were not reporting their conditions. A public awareness campaign about rosacea encouraged people to contact their doctors, which helped to identify more accurately how many people suffer from this condition.

Rosacea is a long-term disease in which dilated blood vessels affect the skin or eyes. It is characterized by skin that is red, pimply, and thickened. The symptoms of **ocular rosacea** may include dry eyes, tearing, sensitivity to light, burning or redness of the eyes, or a feeling as if something gritty is in the eyes. The exact cause of rosacea is not known.

Rosacea that affects the skin can occur anywhere on the body but is most often seen on the face. The frequent flushing of rosacea can cause a painful stinging. In the early stages, redness generally occurs on the center of the face. Dilated blood vessels may become visible and appear as red lines on a reddened face. As rosacea persists, bumps, pustules and eye inflammation may develop. In some cases, mostly in men, an enlarged, bulbous nose, typically red and oily, develops; this condition is known as **rhinophyma**. Those with rhinophyma have enlarged, active oil glands. Identifying the symptoms of

DEPRESSION AND COSMETIC MEDICINE: A CURE?

A recent study by the American Society of Plastic Surgeons shows that plastic surgery procedures can act as a mood enhancer.[20] Researchers interviewed 362 patients, including 61 patients (17 percent) who were taking antidepressants at the time. Within six months after their procedure, 31 percent of the patients taking antidepressants discontinued use of their antidepressants. Of all the patients interviewed, 98 percent said they had an increase in self-esteem. This study may explain more about the motivations of those seeking cosmetic procedures than about cosmetic surgery alleviating depression in the general population.

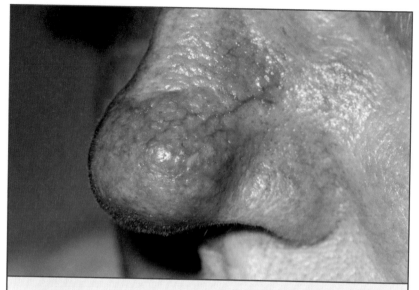

Figure 6.2 This woman's rosacea has led to the formation of a rhinophyma. (© Dr P. Marazzi / Photo Researchers, Inc)

rosacea early on and receiving treatment is important in preventing the later stages of this disease.

Although rosacea does not impose physically debilitating ailments, it affects a patient greatly in an emotional way. In a survey by the National Rosacea Society, nearly 70 percent of patients said the disorder lowered their self-confidence and self-esteem, and 41 percent reported it caused them to avoid public contact or cancel social engagements.

Scientists do not know for certain what causes rosacea although the condition is clearly associated with dilation of the blood vessels. Rosacea is no longer believed to be associated with hormones, as acne is. For people with rosacea, triggers such as heat, exercise, wind, sunlight, and emotional stress can cause flare-ups. Research funded by the University of Utah shows that rosacea patients usually have higher levels of **antigens**, which are molecules that cause an immune response. This suggests that rosacea might be an allergic response. It is also thought that rosacea may occur because of a person's reaction to naturally occurring bacteria that live on the skin or mites that live in oil glands. Another theory holds that the redness and inflammation is caused by a breakdown in connective tissues—such as collagen—that support the blood vessels. As scientists learn more, rosacea appears to differ greatly from adult acne. As a result, this disease is no longer referred to as acne rosacea.

ROSACEA TREATMENTS

Rosacea currently can't be cured, but there are drugs available to control some of its symptoms. Dermatologists often prescribe oral antibiotics to treat the pimples and eye problems. Typical antibiotics include tetracycline, minocycline, erythromycin, and doxycycline. In July 2006, a new oral antibiotic named Oracea was launched to target the bumps and pimples associated with rosacea. The active ingredient in Oracea is doxycycline and the medication is usually taken daily. Oracea contains a dose of doxycycline that does not kill bacteria but rather has an anti-inflammatory effect that works well for rosacea. This drug has been quite popular, with 92,000 prescriptions filled within six months of its launch.

While the pimples associated with rosacea have responded to treatment, other symptoms are not as easy to treat. Flushing and redness are not as influenced by bacteria, and thus will not be helped by antibiotics. Patients with rhinophyma may require surgery to reduce the excess tissue that has developed in the nose area.

Rosacea can also be treated with topical applications, such as creams and gels. Some FDA-approved topical drugs for rosacea are antibiotics (metronidazole, azalaic acid, sodium sulfacetamide, and sulfur) and they have primarily an anti-inflammatory effect. Different products will have varying levels of effectiveness depending on what is triggering the inflammation. If the inflammation is caused by an allergic response to naturally occurring bacteria on the skin, then metronidazole—which has the strongest antibiotic effect—might be a better choice.

7

The Rise of Cosmetic Drugs

The demand for cosmetic drugs is on the rise. The ease of application of these products and increasing affluence of an aging population contribute to the popularity of cosmetic drugs. For many people, a few Botox and Restylane injections are a much-preferred alternative to a face-lift that requires a hospital stay, recovery time, and the potential for surgical complications. Botox and facial fillers are by far the most popular cosmetic drugs, in part because everyone with aging skin is a potential customer. Drug manufacturers have responded to this demand by focusing on new and improved facial fillers.

The most serious downside to the growing popularity of cosmetic drugs is that the increased demand has led to the creation of dangerous impostor drugs and ineffective creams. With so many products to regulate, the FDA works to make sure products are safe but encourages consumers to protect themselves by verifying what they are ingesting or applying.

LONGER-LASTING FILLERS

One trend in facial fillers is longer-lasting products. Bio-Alcamid is a permanent filler that has a consistency similar to human tissue. It is used in more than 20 countries, excluding the United States. Although this filler is not currently approved by the FDA, it is likely to be approved in the future.

Bio-Alcamid works like a surgical implant without being as invasive. It is 96 percent water; the other 4 percent consists of a

long-chained, synthetic compound. The Italian manufacturer, Polymekon Research, claims this compound is safe and
doesn't produce an allergic response. Once the product is
injected, a chemical reaction occurs whereby a thin, natural
capsule is formed, which encloses the substance. The capsule
begins to form within a few days after the injection and is
completed by six weeks. The obvious advantage of this capsule is that it prevents reabsorption into the body, which is
why it is considered permanent.

Despite the fact that it is technically an implant, the
injected area has the look and feel of real tissue if the injection
is a success. The implant can also be easily removed if necessary.
Bio-Alcamid is intended for significant soft tissue loss, such as
that typically seen in those with AIDS, and for deep nasolabial
folds resulting from old age. It is also used to improve the
appearance of congenital deformities, such as chest or breast
irregularities, or deformities from breast augmentations.

Dermalive is a permanent filler that contains particles suspended in a hyaluronic acid base. The particles in the filler are
flexible and consist of acrylic with a high water content. The
water content gives the filler its flexibility and elasticity so that
it can more easily fill wrinkles, folds, and any other depressions
in the face. Two or three treatments can give lasting results to
fill scars, fill nasolabial folds, and enhance cheekbones as well
as chins. DermaLive has a low risk of allergic response, and the
FDA is expected to approve it in the near future.

Approved by the FDA in December 2006, Radiesse is
another facial filler that is longer lasting than most other
nonpermanent fillers currently on the market. It is semipermanent and can contain either calcium hydroxyapatite
or calcium-based microspheres, which are substances that
increase natural collagen production. Radiesse boosts collagen
by creating "scaffolding" that encourages the collagen to grow
around it. This scaffolding is broken down in about a year, but
the natural collagen produced by the body stays. The effects of
this filler are said to last about a year. Radiesse is also used for

vocal chord problems and scars due to radiological treatments. Future uses of this drug may include the treatment of fat loss in HIV patients.

Some fillers under development contain compounds taken from pigs. The fillers Evolence and Evolence Breeze are the first couple of cosmetic products to be sourced from pigs. They contain pig collagen, more delicately referred to as porcine collagen. Evolence and Evolence Breeze are used in Europe, primarily for enhancing facial volume and contours. Evolence Breeze has a lighter density than Evolence, so it is better suited for fine lines and for plumping up the lips. Evolence is better suited for deeper lines and wrinkles. Evolence and Evolence Breeze both last longer than most other collagen injections. Results last approximately 12 months; other fillers typically last 6 months or less. As of October 2007, however, Evolence and Evolence Breeze had not yet been approved by the FDA.

Many more facial fillers are approved in other countries and are pending FDA approval. The trend is toward permanent treatments with a natural look as well as a low allergic response. Many of these fillers contain hyaluronic acid composed of larger particles that enable the product to fill deeper wrinkles and depressions of the cheeks and nasolabial folds. They are not recommended for areas of the face with thin tissue. To increase their longevity, fillers are injected farther into the dermis than other hyaluronic acid products such as Restylane.

BEAUTY AND THE BLACK MARKET

The Kaplans' near-fatal case of botulism from impostor Botox described in Chapter 2 is not the only account of a doctor using imitation Botox. In October 2003, Dr. Stephen L. Seldon began buying a Botox alternative, a product that contained the botulinum toxin A. This impostor Botox, from Arizona-based Toxin Research International, was labeled "For Research Purposes Only." Along with his wife, Dr. Seldon ran a clinic in Las Vegas called A New You Medical Aesthetics and advertised

Botox injections. The couple injected the fake Botox into patients; they were arrested in June 2007 for injecting patients with an unapproved botulinum toxin. Fortunately, as of the writing of this book, there have not been any reports of illness as a result of this case.

Dr. Eric Seiger from The Skin and Vein Center in Michigan was also charged, in 2006, with using drugs that were not FDA approved. One of them, Perlane, is a facial filler not currently approved by the FDA for any purpose in the United States; it is legal for use in Canada, however. While it is likely to be approved in the future, the product remains illegal to use in the United States until that happens. Except for research purposes, products that are not FDA approved can't be imported into the United States by doctors or used on patients.

Beginning in 2003, Dr. Seiger made arrangements for Perlane and Restylane (which had not yet been approved by the FDA but also had been approved in Canada) to be shipped to Windsor, Canada, by the manufacturer. He paid an employee $100 to travel to Windsor to pick up the packages with the instructions to deny any knowledge of the contents if stopped by U.S. Customs.

Eventually Dr. Seiger grew tired of sending the employee to Canada, so he had the packages sent to a dentist there instead. An employee of the dentist then shipped the Perlane and Restylane to Dr. Seiger's offices. When Dr. Seiger needed more Perlane and Restylane, he would call the manufacturer and claim to be a representative of the dentist's office.

According to Michigan's attorney general, on September 2, 2004, officials got warrants to search for the illegal drugs and went to the four business locations of The Skin and Vein Center where Dr. Seiger practiced. The office manager unsuccessfully attempted to hide the Perlane in a locked box while the officials were searching the premises.

Dr. Seiger pleaded guilty to importation of non-FDA-approved medical devices. (Perlane and Restylane are considered medical devices.) His clinics had to pay a penalty

Figure 7.1 Injections of cosmetic drugs meant to shape the face led to pain, swelling, and disfigurement in this woman. *(© AP Images)*

of $412,048.61 to the U.S. government. Dr. Seiger's medical license was not revoked, and he is still a practicing doctor with a Web site that boasts of all his accomplishments and makes no mention of his arrest.

Dr. Seiger is definitely not the only doctor purchasing cosmetic drugs that are not legal in the United States but are legal elsewhere. Before Restylane was approved by the FDA in December 2003, there were reports of doctors traveling to countries where it had been approved to purchase it and bring it back to the United States and of patients traveling to those countries to receive injections.

DRUGS, THE INTERNET, AND THE FDA

Many people today feel comfortable making purchases over the Internet, including of prescription drugs. The Internet serves as a pharmacy that can ship products globally. With new

Internet drug companies popping up almost daily, the FDA warns about the possible dangers of purchasing prescription drugs in this manner.

In 2007, the FDA received complaints that a counterfeit weight-loss drug was sold to three consumers on two different Web sites. The sites claimed to be selling Xenical, an FDA-approved drug meant for obese patients who meet specific height and weight requirements. Lab tests eventually showed that the product sold did not contain any of the active ingredients found in authentic Xenical. Instead, the pills contained the active ingredient sibutramine, which is contained in Meridia, another weight-loss drug. It's impossible to discern whether the pills were inadvertently or intentionally switched. Whatever the case, such a switch can be extremely dangerous to a patient.

The FDA also discovered that other samples from these Web sites contained only talc and starch, despite the fact that the packaging contained a valid lot number. A lot number indicates specifics of where the drug was manufactured. The lot number listed on the drug did not correlate, however, with the true expiration date for that lot. Instead, the expiration was

WHAT IS A CLINICAL TRIAL?

A clinical trial is a research study, using humans, intended to answer health questions. Usually it's part of an effort to get a new drug or drug use approved by the FDA. The researchers are responsible for letting the participants know what risks there could be. The ultimate decision is left up to the patient. Why might someone be willing to be a human guinea pig? Money is one possibility. Another scenario is the patient wants to receive a treatment without having to pay for it, which could be the case with a cosmetic drug. Lastly, a participant could have a disease that has not responded to other drugs and is willing to try something new by way of the clinical trial.

listed as April 2007, whereas the expiration date of the lot was March 2005. Further investigation revealed that these two Web sites, http://www.brandpills.com and http://www.pillspharm .com, had been implicated previously in selling counterfeit drugs to fight avian bird flu. Both of these companies are based outside the United States. The FDA recommends that consumers exercise caution when buying any drugs over the Internet and be particularly wary if there is no way to contact anyone at the Web site by phone or if the drugs seem much cheaper than usual.

Another danger of buying drugs online is that a drug prescription generally requires a trip to a doctor, at least when the medication is first prescribed. The doctor should evaluate the patient to make sure there are no dangers posed to the patient and that the drug does not conflict with any other medications the person is currently taking. Many Internet-based "pharmacies" do not require a prescription. Some Web sites proudly declare this fact. One result has been reports of medications being sold to patients they were not appropriate for and causing heart attacks. Other Web sites require purchasers to fill out a questionnaire and state that answers will be evaluated; however, often there is no proof or information about the identity or qualifications of the reviewer. The safety of the questionnaire method also requires that the person is answering the questions truthfully. But the "correct" answers would be easy to discern for an eager patient wanting to get a weight-loss or hair-loss drug.

In addition to regulating the safety, effectiveness, and manufacturing of pharmaceutical drugs, the FDA also regulates the prescribing process. Specifically, the sale of a prescription drug requires a prescription. The FDA can prohibit Web sites that do not require a prescription from selling to Americans. But since many of these companies are based outside of the United States, the sites can't be shut down entirely.

In response to irresponsible Internet pharmacies, the National Association of Boards of Pharmacy (NABP) got together and developed a certification program to prove which Web sites are legitimate. The NABP was created in the early 1900s to assist states with developing medical licensing standards. This certification program created by NABP requires that the Internet site that sells prescription drugs maintain all state licenses, maintain patient privacy, and allow the National Association of Boards of Pharmacy to inspect its operations. By following these requirements, the Web site can then have this seal—Verified Internet Pharmacy Practice Sites (VIPPS)—on its site with a link to VIPPS so that customers can understand that this site has been reviewed and approved by a group of independent doctors.

WEIGHING THE OPTIONS—AND RISKS

Cosmetic drugs are a popular choice among many people, but they are simply a choice, rather than a necessity. Acne, wrinkles, and baldness have not caused the death of anyone, but drugs to treat these conditions undoubtedly increase quality of life in the minds of consumers. The procedures to apply these cosmetics are becoming more convenient, but the drugs themselves should be evaluated with the same caution as any other drug. A cosmetic drug mislabeled or given to the wrong patient can have disastrous results—as was the case with the Kaplans, who developed botulism and remained incapacitated for many months. When considering a cosmetic drug, cost, safety, permanence, side effects, and experience of the doctor administering the drug should all be evaluated.

Notes

1. Demierre, Marie-France. "Time for the national legislation of indoor tanning to protect minors." *Archives of Dermatology* 13 (2003): 520.

2. Hornung, Robin L., Kristin H. Magee, Willie J. Lee, Lori A. Hansen, and Y-Ching Hsieh. "Tanning facility use: are we exceeding Food and Drug Administration limits?" *Journal of the American Academy of Dermatology* 49 (2003): 655-661.

3. Stehlin, Dori. "Erasing Wrinkles: Easier Said Than Done." *FDA Consumer,* July 1, 1987. Available online. URL: http://findarticles.com/p/articles/mi_m1370/is_v21/ai_5117851. Downloaded May 29, 2007.

4. Carruthers, Alastair. "History." The Carruthers. Available online. URL: http://www.carruthers.net. Downloaded February 24, 2007.

5. Bhutani, Mohit, Edward Ralph, and Michael D. Sharpe. "Acute paralysis following 'a bad potato': a case of botulism." *Canadian Journal of Anesthesia* 52, 4 (2005): 433-436.

6. Centers for Disease Control and Prevention. "Botulism Outbreak Associated with Eating Fermented Food–Alaska, 2001." *Morbidity and Mortality Weekly Report,* 32 (August 17, 2001): 680-682.

7. Lamas, Daniela. "Doctors Skeptical about Botox-type Creams." *The Miami Herald,* October 3, 2003. Available online. URL: http://www.accessmylibrary.com/coms2/summary_0286-8136218_ITM. Downloaded July 5, 2007.

8. Moore, Andre. "The biochemistry of beauty." *European Molecular Biology Organization, EMBO Reports,* 3, 8 (2002): 714.

9. Kane, Michael. *The Botox Book.* New York, NY: St. Martin's Press, 2002, 135.

10. Howard Hughes Medical Institute. Biosingularity. "Researchers discover botulism toxin's insidious route into nerve cells." Updated March 19, 2006. Available online. URL: http://biosingularity.wordpress.com/2006/03/19/researchers-discover-botulism-toxins-insidious-route-into-nerve-cells/. Downloaded May 5, 2007.

11. Burgess, Cheryl M. "Soft tissue augmentation in skin of color: market growth, available fillers, and successful techniques." *Journal of Drugs in Dermatology* 6, 1 (January 2007): 51.

12. Carruthers, Alistair. "Hyaluronic acid gel in skin rejuvenation." *Journal of Drugs in Dermatology* 5, 10 (Nov.-Dec. 2006): 959-964.

13. Reilly, Colleen. "Antioxidants and Skin Care: Media Hype or Wonder Drug?" The Health Psychology Home Page, Vanderbilt University. Available online. URL: http://www.vanderbilt.edu. Downloaded May 15, 2007.

14. Brannon, Heather. "Alpha Hydroxy Acids." Your Guide to Beauty. Available online. URL: www.dermatology.about.com. Downloaded May 1, 2007.

15. Kuechel, Marie C. "Can Peels Prevent Cancer?" *New Beauty,* June/July 2007, 35.

16. Rao, Jaggi, Kristina E. Paabo, and Mitchel P. Goldman. "A double-blinded randomized trial testing the tolerability and efficacy of a novel topical agent with and without occlusion for the treatment of cellulite: a study and review of the literature." *Journal of Drugs in Dermatology* 3, 4 (July 2004): 419.

17. Federal Trade Commission. "FTC Charges Marketer of 'CPM' Tablets with Making Unsubstantiated Weight-Loss Claims." FTC Press Release. November 27, 1991. Available online. URL: http://www.ftc.gov. Downloaded June 2, 2007.

18. Iowa Attorney General. "Lipo Slim Briefs: Not Available in Iowa." Press Release. March 10, 1999. Available online. URL: http://www.state.ia.us. Downloaded June 1, 2007.

19. Fischer, David. "The Bald Truth." *U.S. News and World Report,* August 4, 1997. Available online. URL:

http://www.usnews.com/usnews/biz-tech/articles/970804/archive_007580.htm. Downloaded July 23, 2007.

20. Kuechel, Marie C. "Surgical Mood Boosters." *New Beauty,* June/July 2007, 37.

Glossary

acetylcholine—A neurotransmitter that relays information in the brain that controls muscle contraction. Botox inhibits acetylcholine thereby preventing the muscles from contracting.

alkaloid—A chemical found naturally in certain plants that has been used historically as a sedative, poison, and as an antidote to other poisons.

alpha hydroxy acid—A chemical found naturally in fruits, vegetables, and milk sugars that some people believe can slow the aging process.

androgens—Male hormones in men and women that can cause acne.

antidote—A medication used to counteract the effect of a poison.

antigens—Molecules that cause an immune response.

antioxidants—Chemicals that boost collagen production and strengthen blood vessels.

Bell's palsy—A condition in which people temporarily lose all control of facial muscles on one side of the face.

botulinum toxin A—A toxin produced by the bacterium *Clostridium botulinum* and the active ingredient in Botox.

botulism—The disease caused by a nerve toxin produced from the spore-forming bacterium *Clostridium botulinum*.

bovine-based—Derived from cows.

bronchodilator—A drug that opens lung passageways.

carcinogen—Something that causes cancer, such as UV radiation from sunlight.

cell—The basic unit of living things.

collagen—A long, fibrous protein that provides structure to cells that make up skin, cartilage, tendons, and bone.

cosmeceuticals—Cosmetics that have medicinal benefits, such as improving wrinkles, acne, and pigmentation problems.

cosmetic drug—A product that is intended to be rubbed, poured, sprinkled, or sprayed on, or otherwise applied to the human body for cleansing, beautifying, or altering the appearance, as well as helping to treat, prevent, or mitigate a disease.

cosmetic—An article intended to be rubbed, poured, sprinkled, or sprayed on, or otherwise applied to the human body for cleansing, beautifying, or altering the appearance.

dermis—The layer of skin beneath the epidermis that cushions the body from strain.

dihydrotestosterone (DHT)—An enzyme that reacts with testosterone in the hair follicle, which creates a byproduct that dries up the hair follicle.

DNA (deoxyribonucleic acid)—A molecule containing the genetic instructions for the cells of living organisms.

elastic fibers—Proteins in skin that provide elasticity in connective tissues.

enzyme—A protein that accelerates a chemical reaction.

epidermis—The outermost layer of the skin.

estrogen—A hormone produced by the ovaries to support female sex characteristics.

exfoliation—The process of removing old skin cells to encourage the growth of new cells.

facial fillers—Cosmetic drugs that are injected deep within the dermis to add volume and contour to skin.

finasteride—The active ingredient in Propecia that treats hair loss in men by inhibiting the formation of DHT, which dries up the hair follicle.

free radicals—Unstable molecules that damage cells and possibly prevent their normal functioning.

granulomas—Tiny bumps caused by facial fillers that can be felt, and sometimes seen, under the skin.

melanin—A pigment in the skin that protects the body from UV radiation.

mesotherapy—The process of injecting drugs deep within the skin to reduce the appearance of cellulite.

microbial resistance—Occurs when bacteria have altered genetically and no longer die from exposure to an antibiotic.

neocollagenesis—Renewed production of collagen by the body as a result of a Botox or facial filler injection.

neurotransmitter—A chemical that communicates information between neurons.

ocular rosacea—A disease that causes dry eyes, tearing, redness, burning, or a feeling that something gritty is in the eyes.

off-label—A drug being used legally for a purpose not approved by the FDA.

orphan drug—A status designated by the FDA for drugs that treat diseases affecting fewer than 200,000 Americans.

photoaging—The aging of the skin from the sun.

PLLA—A biodegradable, semipermanent filler that is currently being used primarily for HIV-related loss of facial fat under the trade name Sculptra.

retinoids—Topical agents that stimulate new growth of tiny blood vessels, which regenerates skin cell growth in the treatment of acne and wrinkles.

rhinophyma—A condition associated with rosacea that is characterized by an enlarged, bulbous, typically red and oily nose.

Glossary

rosacea—A chronic inflammation of the skin, usually affecting the face but sometimes other areas.

sebum—Oil produced from glands in the dermis.

subcutaneous layer—The fatty region below the dermis that attaches the skin to underlying bone and muscle.

sudden infant death syndrome (SIDS)—The death of infants under the age of 12 months during sleep caused by a cessation of breathing. The causes remain somewhat unclear; One possibility is infant botulism.

trade name—A name for a specific product brand. Colgate is a trade name for a type of toothpaste. Botox is also a trade name.

type C botulism—A type of potentially fatal food poisoning that occurs in animals that eat insects or animals containing the toxin from the strain of *Clostridium botulinum* that produces Type C botulinum toxin.

wnts—Proteins that create new hair follicles.

Bibliography

American Academy of Otolaryngology – Head and Neck Surgery (AAO-HNS). "Bell's Palsy." AAO-HNS on the Web. Available online. URL: http://www.entnet.org/healthinfo/topics/bells.cfm. Downloaded July 9, 2007.

Associated Press. "Doctor, Wife Charged with Injecting Patients with Toxin Instead of Botox." *Bucks County Courier Times,* June 29, 2007, 9A.

Atkinson, Louise and Linda Gray. "This Woman Endured Five Days of Hell Having Her Face 'Peeled' with Acid." *Evening Standard,* February 12, 2002. Available online. URL: http://www.highbeam.com. Downloaded July 5, 2007.

Baldauf, Sarah. "Beyond Wrinkles." *U.S. News and World Report,* January 22, 2007. Available online. URL: http://www.usnews.com. Downloaded August 13, 2007.

Barash, Jason, Tania W.H. Tang, and Stephen S. Arnon. "First case of infant botulism caused by *Clostridium baratii* Type F in California." *Journal of Clinical Microbiology* 43, 8 (August 2005): 4280-4282.

Berschler, Susan P. "The Changing Face of Cosmetic Enhancement." *Lifestyle,* June 2007, 36-41.

Ciavaglia, Jo. "A New Wrinkle: Fountain of Youth in a Syringe?" *Bucks County Courier Times,* February 21, 2007, 1A-2A.

Centers for Disease Control and Prevention. "Botulism outbreak associated with eating fermented food—Alaska, 2001." *Morbidity and Mortality Weekly Report* 50, 32 (August 17, 2001): 680-682.

Debree, Crissa S. "Skin Drug Boosts CollaGenex." *Bucks County Courier Times.* August 8, 2007, 1B-4B.

Demierre, Marie-France. "Time for the national legislation of indoor tanning to protect minors." *Archives of Dermatology* 13 (2003): 520.

Hanke, William C. "A protocol for facial volume restoration with poly-L-lactic acid." *Journal of Drugs in Dermatology* 5, 9 (October 2006): 972-877.

Henkel, John. "Buying Drugs Online: It's Convenient and Private, but Beware of 'Rogue Sites.'" *FDA Consumer.* Available online. URL: http://www.fda.gov. Downloaded August 5, 2007.

_____ "Indoor tanning—magnitude of the health issue." *Journal of Drugs in Dermatology* 5, 2 (Feb. 1, 2006): 193-195.

Leon, Vicki. *Working IX to V in Ancient Rome and Greece.* New York, NY: Walker & Company, 2007.

NBC 6. "Doctor Sentenced to Three Years in Fake Botox Case." NBC 6 Live Online South Florida. Available online. URL: http://www.nbc6.net/news. Downloaded August 31, 2007.

Bibliography

NBC 6. "Girlfriend Sues Doctor Over Botched Botox Injection." *NBC 6 Live Online South Florida*. Available online. URL: http://www.nbc6.net/news. Downloaded August 31, 2007.

NBC 6. "Investigation Continues into Botox-Botulism Cases." *NBC 6 Live Online South Florida*. Available online. URL: http://www.nbc6.net/news. Downloaded August 31, 2007.

Pitman, Simon. "Scientists Discover Small Molecules Up Botox Efficacy." Decision News Media SAS. Available online. URL: http://www.cosmeticdesign-europe.com. Downloaded March 3, 2007.

Singer, Natasha. "Feel Pudgy? There's a Shot for That." *The New York Times*. Available online. URL: http://www.nytimes.com. Downloaded October 3, 2007.

University of Michigan Health System. "Science Behind a Wrinkle-Filler: Researchers Discover For First Time How Product Works," *ScienceDaily*. Available online. URL: http://www.sciencedaily.com. Posted on February 20, 2007.

U.S. Department of Justice. "Skin and Vein Center Pleads Guilty to Importation of Non-FDA Approved Medical Devices." Press Release. July 10, 2006. Available online. URL: http://www.usdoj.gov/usao/mie/press/2006/2006-07-10_eseiger.pdf. Downloaded September 11, 2007.

Rush PR News. "FDA Warns Consumers about Buying Drugs Online." May 12, 2007. Available online. URL: http://www.rushprnews.com. Downloaded August 5, 2007.

Rodgers, Elaine. "Vanity: Our Old Friend." *Solutions at Home – Philadelphia*, June 2007, 34-36.

Further Reading

Books

Kane, Michael. *The Botox Book.* New York: St. Martin's Press, 2002.

Libal, Autumn. *Can I Change the Way I Look? A Teen's Guide to the Health Implications of Cosmetic Surgery, Makeovers and Beyond.* Broomall, Penn.: Mason Crest Publishers, 2004.

Sheen, Barbara. *Diseases and Disorders—Acne.* Farmington Hills, Mich.: Lucent Publishers, 2004.

Web Sites

AcneNet—American Academy of Dermatology's online resource for causes and treatment for acne.
http://www.skincarephysicians.com/acnenet

Centers for Disease Control and Prevention (CDC)—Information about botulism and proper canning.
http://www.cdc.gov

Consumer Reports—Information and evaluation of products, including cosmetics.
http://www.consumerreports.org

Drug Digest—Consumer health and drug information.
http://www.drugdigest.org

eMedicineHealth—Consumer health information written by physicians for consumers.
http://www.emedicinehealth.com

International Rosacea Foundation—Causes, research, and treatment for rosacea sufferers.
http://www.internationalrosaceafoundation.org

International Society of Cosmetogyncecology—An association of gynecologic specialists in female cosmetic surgery and medicine.
http://www.iscgyn.com

Quackwatch—Health fraud information.
http://www.quackwatch.org

Science Daily—Research news on various science topics including cosmetic drugs.
http://www.sciencedaily.com

Further Reading

U.S. Food and Drug Administration (FDA)—Regulations, research, and news on drugs and cosmetics.
http://www.cfsan.fda.gov

U.S. National Library of Medicine—National Institutes of Health—Current health news.
http://www.nlm.nih.gov

Index

Index

Index

peels. *See* chemical peels; hydroxy acids and chemical peels
periodontal disease, 12
Perlane, 83
phenol peels, 59–60
phosphatidylcholine deoxycholate (PCDC), 65
photoaging, 21
pigmentation problems. *See* skin, coloring problems
pills for hair loss, 69–70
PLLA (poly-l-lactic acid), 46, 52–53
poly-l-lactic acid. *See* PLLA
porcine collagen, 82
pores, 16
Powderz Inc., 44
prescription, 86
prescription drugs, 10, 86
Propecia, 67, 70, 71
Propionibacterium acnes (*P. acnes*), 72, 75
psoriasis, 12
pupils, dilating, 13

Radiesse, 81–82
Rehm, Diane, 33
Renaissance women, 13
research, drug, 24–25
Restylane, 51–52, 80, 83–84
retinoids (tretinoin), 54–55, 75
Retinol, 63. *See also* retinoids
rhinophyma, 77, 78
rickets, 21
Rogaine, 69
Romans, 13
rosacea
described, 76–79
self-esteem, 72
treatment, 15, 79

salicylic acid, 57, 74–75. *See also* beta hydroxy acids
Salvarsan, 6
scanning electron micro-

graph (SEM), 48
scars
acne, 72
minimizing, 33, 34–35
Scripps Research Institute, 41
Sculptra, 52
sebaceous glands, 74
sebum, 72
Seiger, Eric, 83–84
Seldon, Stephen L., 82–84
self-confidence, 78
self-esteem, 72, 77–78
SEM. *See* scanning electron micrograph
Serutox, 36
sibutramine, 85
SIDS. *See* sudden infant death syndrome
skin. *See also* tanning
aging process, 12, 16–23, 46
cancer, 19, 21, 60, 67
cell. *See* cell, skin
coloring problems, 10
complexion, 14
elasticity, 20
function, 16
healing, 12
layers, 16–18
sunlight damage, 19–23
ultraviolet radiation, 18–20
volume, 46
Skin and Vein Center, 83
Slender You, Inc., 64
smoker's mouth, 20
smoking and free radicals, 55
Society of Plastic Surgeons, 77
sodium sulfacetamide, 79
soft tissue augmentation. *See* facial fillers
spasmodic dysphonia, 33
stroke victims, 43
subcutaneous layer, 17–18
sudden infant death syndrome (SIDS), 30

sulfur, 79
sunlight
chemical peels, 58
damage to skin, 19–23, 55
sunscreen
broad-spectrum, 22
cosmetic drug, 10
SPF, 21, 75
sweating, stopping, 33–34

tanning, 18–19. *See also* indoor tanning; skin
phenol peels, 59–60
TCA (trichloroacetic acid) peels, 59, 60, 61
tea tree oil, 12
testosterone and hair loss, 68
tetracyclines, 76, 79
tolerance, drug, 39
topical wrinkle reducers. *See* facial wrinkling, reducers
Toxin Research International, 44, 82
tretinoin. *See* retinoids
trichloroacetic acid peels. *See* TCA peels
Type C botulism, 30–31

ultraviolet radiation (UV), 18–20, 21
University of Miami, 36
University of Pennsylvania, 70
University of Utah, 78
Upjohn, 69
U.S. Food and Drug Administration (FDA)
approval of
Botox, 25, 35
collagen as filler, 49
Restylane, 84
Rogaine, 69
rosacea drugs, 76, 79
Xenical, 85
clinical trial, 85
concerns over

About the Author

Suellen May is a writer living in Bucks County, Pennsylvania. She received a B.S. from University of Vermont and a M.S. from Colorado State University. She writes science-related books and magazine articles, and recently published a five-book environmental series titled *Invasive Species*.

About the Editor

David J. Triggle is a University Professor and a Distinguished Professor in the School of Pharmacy and Pharmaceutical Sciences at the State University of New York at Buffalo. He studied in the United Kingdom and earned his B.Sc. degree in chemistry from the University of Southampton and a Ph.D. in chemistry at the University of Hull. Following post-doctoral work at the University of Ottawa in Canada and the University of London in the United Kingdom, he assumed a position at the School of Pharmacy at Buffalo. He served as chairman of the department of biochemical pharmacology from 1971 to 1985, and as dean of the School of Pharmacy from 1985 to 1995. From 1995 to 2001, he served as the dean of the graduate school and as the university provost from 2000 to 2001. He is the author of several books dealing with the chemical pharmacology of the autonomic nervous system and drug-receptor interactions, some 400 scientific publications, and has delivered more than 1,000 lectures worldwide on his research.